Twayne's English Authors Series

Sylvia E. Bowman, *Editor*

INDIANA UNIVERSITY

Erasmus Darwin

 **160**

Erasmus Darwin

By DONALD M. HASSLER

Kent State University

Twayne Publishers, Inc.   : :   New York

For my Father,
Whose name I sign
Intentionally as mine

Preface

Erasmus Darwin was an active thinker who practiced medicine in provincial England during the second half of the eighteenth century, and it is difficult to place him in the history of English literature because he was so much more than a London literary man. To anyone who takes the time to find and glance through his two volume medical treatise *Zoonomia* and to glance through some of the scientific writings of the French *philosophes,* Darwin seems more akin to prerevolutionary Paris than to London. His intellectual interests were encyclopedic; and, like the writers of the first French *encyclopédie,* he was fascinated by technology and invention and was one of the founders of the famous Lunar Society of Birmingham whose members included James Watt and Matthew Boulton, the men who developed and manufactured the steam engine.[1]

Darwin was also active in the literary circle in Lichfield that included Anna Seward; and, beginning in 1789, he published poems that gained him immediate and wide literary fame. His poems have since fallen out of favor, and he is generally considered a bad poet now primarily because his success was followed so quickly by the Romantic revolution in style. In fact, William Wordsworth's *Preface to the Lyrical Ballads of 1800* was in part a very successful defence of himself against the poetic theory and style of Darwin. In any case, Darwin's poetry, as well as his prose, had a significant influence on the English Romantics.

My purpose in this book is to study Darwin the writer—not the scientist, the doctor, the inventor—and to reassess his total accomplishment as a writer. It will be necessary, however, in my first chapter to explain his ideas and the climate of opinion out of which they grew because his style of writing, particularly his poetic style, is formed from the implications of these ideas. Some are scientific ideas, or more accurately, hypotheses about cosmogony, the study of the origin of the physical world. In a book of this length, I cannot try to discuss the validity of these hypotheses according to our current thinking; but, in Chapter 1, I sketch the outlines of Darwin's philosophic materialism, his comic view of life that this produced, and the resulting effects in his style of writing. In order to do so, it will be necessary to quote some of his prose to illustrate his ideas before describing the works themselves in which the quotations appear either as notes to poems or as part of prose exposition. Similarly, several of Darwin's important over-all literary effects (his comic tone, for instance) are discussed in the long opening chapter, before his individual works are separately described, because the reader needs to be given these frames of reference before he can see the works. Also, as with the content ideas, to which they are related, these overall literary effects may be what is most important in Darwin's work.

The middle chapters of the book give a thorough description and analysis of all his writings as individual works, as he published them. Since all of them are virtually unknown and out of print (recently selections have been reprinted),[2] I have had to paraphrase or to quote more than is customary in discussing more famous works. (In quoting from Darwin's poetry and prose, I have retained his punctuation and habit of capitalizing whole words in order to capture some of the flavor of his expression.) But the liberty is also taken of omitting reference to every small detail in the works in order to allow them to come alive as an exciting, relatively well-unified body of work. On the basis of this analysis of Darwin's works, the last chapter presents my reassessment of him as a writer by showing how he influenced the Romantic poets. There must have been something coherent and powerful in his writings because each of the major Romantics were both frightened and fascinated by Darwin, and this coherence and this power, which exists perhaps more in idea than in artistic unity, are the subject of this book.

Finally, it gives me great pleasure to acknowledge and thank those to whom I am indebted in this project. Professors Marshall Suther and Carl Woodring gave me invaluable direction in my Columbia dissertation on Darwin, but Irwin Primer and Desmond King-Hele have given me advice and encouragement in this later Darwin project. To the English Department of Kent State University I am indebted for reduced teaching loads in the winter and spring of 1969 so that I could complete the manuscript; and *The Serif,* the Kent State University Library Journal, has kindly given me permission to reprint sections from an article entitled "Erasmus Darwin's Comic Bathos." To my wife I am continuously indebted for her patience during this "second dissertation" and to my Aunt, Helen Hassler, for her skillful typing.

DONALD M. HASSLER

Kent, Ohio

Contents

Chronology

1731   Erasmus Darwin born at Elston Hall outside of Nottingham on December 12.

1741-   Student at Chesterfield School.
1750

1750   Enters St. John's College, Cambridge, on an Exeter scholarship.

1751   "The Death of Prince Frederick," his first published poem, in a student volume; republished in *European Magazine* (February, 1795). He also publishes a poem in praise of Thomas Gurney's system of shorthand in the second edition of Gurney's *Brachygraphy* (1751-52). After this, he does not publish a poem until 1789 for fear of damaging his professional reputation as a doctor.

1754   Takes Bachelor of Arts degree; goes to Edinburgh to study medicine.

1755   Returns to Cambridge and takes his Bachelor of Medicine degree; returns to Edinburgh for a brief time.

1756   Begins medical practice in Nottingham; after eight unsuccessful weeks moves to Lichfield (November) and begins very successful practice.

1757   Marries Mary Howard of Lichfield (December). His first paper in the *Philosophical Transactions* of the Royal Society published; he publishes four others in time.

1758   Settles in a comfortable house near the Cathedral in Lichfield; birth of son Charles.

1759   Birth of son Erasmus.

1760   Begins correspondence and long friendship with Matthew Boulton, owner of Soho Ironworks in Birmingham; this friendship and mutual interest in science and technology became the nucleus of the Lunar Society.

1761   Elected Fellow of the Royal Society (April 9).

1763   Birth of daughter Elizabeth; dies in infancy.

1766   Birth of son Robert Waring, the father of the nineteenth-century biologist, Charles Robert Darwin. Meets Jean Jacques Rousseau at Wooton Hall; discusses botany with him; they exchange letters in the next several years.

1767   Birth of son William; dies in infancy.

1768   Kneecap broken in a fall from an invention he was testing; the injury results in a slight limp the rest of his life.

1770   Death of wife, Mary Howard Darwin.

1771-   Fathers two illegitimate daughters by a "Miss Parker."
1778

1771 *Zoonomia* begun.

1774 Samuel Johnson and Mrs. Thrale entertained for breakfast at his house in Lichfield (July 8).

1775 Lunar Society met formally for first time (December 31); meetings held off and on through the 1790's; members included Darwin, Boulton, James Watt, Josiah Wedgwood, Joseph Priestly.

1777 Botanic garden about a mile from Lichfield purchased; poem by that name begun following a suggestion by Anna Seward.

1778 Death of oldest son, Charles, at medical school in Edinburgh from an infection caused by dissecting. Called in to treat the children of Colonel Chandos Pole of Derby and falls in love with his wife; several poems on his unrequited love written in the next few years.

1779- Several attacks of gout suffered; gives up drinking all fermented
1780 liquors and restores his health.

1780 Edits his late son's medical dissertation. Death of Colonel Pole; Darwin, along with numerous other suitors, woos Mrs. Pole.

1781 Marries Mrs. Pole; seven children from his second marriage: the last, a daughter, born 1790. Moves to Derby.

1783 Edits the first of several publications of the Botanical Society at Lichfield which he founded, a translation of Linnaeus.

1784 "The Loves of the Plants," Part II of *Botanic Garden,* sent to London publisher Joseph Johnson who begins negotiations; but Darwin is hesitant to publish because of fears about its reception.

1789 "The Loves of the Plants" published; it is well received.

1790 Popularity so great that he corresponds with Parliament about the possibility of the Poet Laureateship.

1791 *Botanic Garden,* including Part I, "The Economy of Vegetation," published.

1794 *Zoonomia,* Volume I, a prose work on the physical nature of human life.

1796 *Zoonomia,* Volume II, the classification, descriptions, and suggested cures for all human diseases. Samuel Taylor Coleridge visits Darwin in Derby and is chided about religion.

1797 *A Plan for the Conduct of Female Education in Boarding Schools;* his two illegitimate daughters, the "Miss Parkers," ran a girls boarding school.

1799 Death of his second son, Erasmus, by suicide. Darwin takes over his dead son's house, Breadsall Priory, just outside Derby.

1800 *Phytologia, or the Philosophy of Agriculture and Gardening,* the counterpart to *Zoonomia* dealing with plant life and disease rather than human life.

1801 Suffers a dangerous illness brought on by a visit to a patient.

1802 Death of Erasmus Darwin (April 18).

1803 *The Temple of Nature,* his third long poem, published posthumously.

CHAPTER 1

The Milieu of the Philosophes

IN order to understand what Erasmus Darwin wrote and, in particular, the kind of poetry he wrote, it is necessary to understand in what way he was a philosopher. Since the time of Francis Bacon, the proper study of the philosopher had been the book of nature, or natural philosophy; but only during the French Enlightenment did science and daring thinking combine to produce the eighteenth-century phenomenon called the *philosophe*. Although the word is French, the type was international; for its pioneers had been the great Englishmen, Francis Bacon, Isaac Newton, and John Locke; and, according to Peter Gay's recent account of the Enlightenment, a Scotsman, David Hume, became the most daring speculative thinker of them all.[1] But French thinkers, fighting a holy war against a stubbornly entrenched religion, formed the main body of this little army of philosophers. A survey of Darwin's footnotes shows that he acknowledged indebtedness to nearly all of the French *philosophes* as well as to the Englishmen. Notable exceptions are Julien Offray de la Mettrie and Denis Diderot (some of the latter's scientific writings were not published until the nineteenth century). It is sufficient here, however, to explain the content and mood of Darwin's ideas and not to establish indisputable indebtedness, which in any case may be impossible.

The philosophers were dedicated to the principles of analysis and experimentation as they understood them from Bacon and Locke, but they also jumped quickly to broad hypotheses about nature. They were looking for a comprehensive world view in nature to replace the supernatural world view that they thought they were destroying: "Thus speculation centered upon the energy of life and its analogies to other energies and upon those relationships among life forms which might betray a unified system of nature."[2] Darwin's natural philosophy, studded with fascinating detail but also extravagantly theoretical, is a product of this tradition.

I *Analysis and an Imaginative World View*

A convenient bench mark in Darwin's career is the fact that he started medical practice the same year that the book that was to become his most frequent reference on matters of anatomy and physiology was published. Albrecht von Haller's *Elementa physiologiae* (1757–66) collected the results of experiments by the foremost anatomist of the time; Diderot studied it carefully; La Mettrie dedicated his most radical treatise on the mechanical nature of the human body to Haller.[3] And Darwin was to use these results in his own experiments and speculations, for Haller is cited again and again in *Zoonomia.* Darwin did not rely, however, exclusively on secondary material; a notice in the Birmingham newspaper gives a sense of how he got his ideas: "October 23rd, 1762—The body of the Malefactor, who is order'd to be executed at Lichfield on Monday the 25th instant, will be afterwards conveyed to the house of Dr. Darwin, who will begin a Course of Anatomical Lectures, at Four o'clock on Tuesday evening, and continue them every Day as long as the Body can be preserved, and shall be glad to be favoured with the Company of any who profess Medicine or Surgery, or whom the Love of Science may induce."[4]

The habit of analysis—the reduction of every complex into its component parts in order to see it better and to control it—had been turned into a method of thinking by Locke. Darwin accepts this method of analysis completely and continually pays homage to Locke. In *Zoonomia,* Darwin even credits Locke with clear thinking about how to analyze and control toilet habits: "Hence one method of correcting costiveness is by endeavoring to establish a habit of evacuation at a certain hour of the day, as recommended by Mr. Locke, which may be accomplished by using daily voluntary efforts at those times, joined with the ususal stimulus of the material to be evacuated."[5]

The implications of this method of analysis are important in understanding Darwin's thought because even though he was a firm Lockean thinker, the limitations of the method justified and stimulated the other side of Darwin's thought: his wild theorizing or, as Coleridge called it, "Darwinizing."[6] Just as the empiricism of the day demanded dissection in order to see more clearly, so this method of analysis was a reductive way of thinking in which complex ideas (Locke's term) are broken down into simpler ideas in order to see them more clearly. This method was useful because it did away with the "ghosts" of unanalyzable and innate ideas. In the associationist language of David Hartley, who most thoroughly explored this psychology in the eighteenth century, all mental states, including emotions, are "aggregates of simple ideas united by association."[7] But ultimately all simple ideas themselves must be seen as aggregates of still simpler ideas. For example, any sense perception, such as a visual image, can be reduced to several perceptions if more or less time is spent looking or if the space relationships are altered, such as with a microscope.

Bishop Berkeley, the most successful critic of Locke's methodology, pointed out the impossibility of ever getting down to the basic simple ideas; and Darwin seems to be fully aware of the problem while, at the same time, he accepts the analytic method of Locke and Hartley as the only effective method for "seeing" ideas: "So that though our visible ideas resemble in miniature the outline of the figure of coloured bodies, in other respects they serve only as a language, which by acquired associations introduce the tangible ideas of bodies. Hence it is, that this sense is so readily deceived by the art of the painter to our amusement and instruction. The reader will find much very curious knowledge on this subject in Bishop Berkeley's Essay on Vision, a work of great ingenuity."[8]

Visual images are all-important in this analytic method of the Enlightenment because "clear thinking" is a direct result of reducing complexity to nonmisty outlines that can be "seen." Hence the name "Enlightenment" stems directly from Locke.[9] In addition to the puzzling fact that ultimate particles can never be seen, or perhaps because of this fact, language is arbitrary and can only approximate its subject. Locke, who had devoted the third book of his *Essay Concerning Human Understanding* to this problem, had concluded not only that words are arbitrary but that all substantive words are general. This conclusion would follow, of course, since, if final particular particles can never be reached by reductive analysis, they could hardly be named by the arbitrary signs that are used to refer to the analysis. Thus, the language of Lockean analysis has to be one of vivid, visual imagery in which the ideas imaged are never completely seen but only approximated; and Darwin again seems to understand and to accept the implications: "Mr. Locke observes, that languages consist principally of general terms; as it would have been impossible to give a name to every

individual object, so as to communicate an idea of it to others;
it would be like reciting the name of every individual soldier of
an army, instead of using the general term, army."[10]

Perhaps these limitations, inherent in the Lockean methodology,
encouraged speculation. Caught in what seemed like an infinite
regress of analysis and definition, any serious Lockean had to
supply connections and names in order to stop his analysis from
spiraling down to a world of infinitely subdividable simple ideas.
For example, in *Zoonomia*, Darwin tries to analyze associations
down to firm statements about the physiology of nerves (which
psychologists are still trying to do); and he has to give a name to
one of the steps in his analysis. But he makes it quite clear that the
name is only a name, and hence tentative: "therefore the particles
of the muscular fibre (which in its state of relaxation are supposed
not to touch) cannot affect each other without the influence of
some intermediate agent; this agent is here termed the spirit of
animation, or sensorial power, but may with equal propriety be
termed the power, which causes contraction; or may be called by
any other name, which the reader may choose to affix to it."[11]

Darwin does not insist on any innate or supernatural validity
to "the spirit of animation"; he simply names something that might
exist so that he can continue to analyze it to *see* if it exists. Thus,
the imaginative giving of names, or speculation in the literal sense
of "seeing," was the logical counterpart to Lockean analysis. However, Darwin was apparently more gifted with a talent for speculative image-making than for analysis. In a letter to Darwin's son
(Charles Darwin's father), James Keir describes this talent: "Your
father paid little regard to authority, and he quickly perceived the
analogies on which a new theory could be founded. This penetration
or sagacity by which he was able to discover very remote causes
and distant effects, was the characteristic of his understanding."[12]

Darwin's own statement of the need for theorizing is firm and
appears at the beginning of his longest theoretical treatise, *Zoonomia:* "There are some modern practitioners, who declaim against
medical theory in general, not considering that to think is to theorize;
and that no one can direct a method of cure to a person labouring
under disease without thinking, that is, without theorizing; and
happy therefore is the patient, whose physician possesses the best
theory."[13]

The "best" theory, which runs continually through Darwin's

writings, is one of material forces moving inexorably over vast distances of time and space, with no supernatural or anthropomorphic agency, to produce nearly infinite configurations of organic and inorganic matter. In short, Darwin was a materialist with a profound sense of change and flux. Speculation of this sort was not invented, of course, by the iconoclastic *philosophes;* for the concept goes back through Lucretius and Epicurus to the pre-Socratic philosophers.[14] Not until the nineteenth century, however, was convincing evidence found to establish this monistic world view of material forces that move independently over vast distances of time and space as much more than a speculation. But the vision was there among the *philosophes;* and passages from La Mettrie, Diderot, Buffon, Holbach, Godwin, and Darwin are particularly eloquent expressions of materialism.

A crucial point in any vision of materialism has to do with the transition from inorganic to organic matter. The most speculative eighteenth-century physiologists, including La Mettrie and Darwin, thought that all mental activity could be explained by the movement of physical parts; but the question was how matter could acquire "animal motion" in the first place. Numerous experiments were devised to establish proof for the spontaneous generation of life from nonliving material, and Darwin thought some of them were nearly conclusive. His comments on this subject are cautious, and he pays lip service to what he calls "spirit," as well as to an original divine creator of "Parent of Parents." But the weight of his interest seems to be on the self-sufficiency of the material world to create life and to create it abundantly:

From the misconception of the ignorant or superstitious, it has been thought somewhat profane to speak in favour of spontaneous vital production, as if it contradicted holy writ. . . . It was not considered, that animals and vegetables have been perpetually improving by reproduction; and that spontaneous vitality was only to be looked for in the simplest organic beings, as in the smallest microscopic animalcules. . . .

But it may appear too bold in the present state of our knowledge on this subject, to suppose that all vegetables and animals now existing were originally derived from the smallest microscopic ones, formed by spontaneous vitality; and that they have, by innumerable reproductions, during innumerable centuries of time, gradually acquired the size, strength, and excellence of form and faculties which they now possess; and that such amazing powers were originally impressed on matter and spirit by the great Parent of Parents, Cause of Causes, Ens Entinum![15]

Given the power of spontaneous generation, then, matter is capable of infinite variations and improvements over adequate periods of time and space. On this point Darwin begins to anticipate modern theories of evolution although he did not accumulate the physical evidence that his grandson did, nor did he sense the importance of random mutations in evolutionary change.[16] In the section "On Generation" in *Zoonomia,* he prudently evades a firm statement on spontaneous generation; but he argues at great length that animals are able to pass on physical changes to their offspring and that continual regeneration along these lines has produced all varieties of life from one original life source. A long passage from the conclusion to Darwin's argument in *Zoonomia* illustrates Darwin's emphasis on vast time and on material forces:

From thus meditating on the great similarity of the structure of the warm-blooded animals, and at the same time of the great changes they undergo both before and after their nativity; and by considering in how minute a portion of time many of the changes of animals above described have been produced; would it be too bold to imagine, that in the great length of time, since the earth began to exist, perhaps millions of ages before the commencement of the history of mankind, would it be too bold to imagine, that all warm-blooded animals have arisen from one living filament, which the Great First Cause endued with animality, with the power of acquiring new parts, attended with new propensities, directed by irritations, sensations, volitions, and associations; and thus possessing the faculty of continuing to improve by its own inherent activity, and of delivering down those improvements by generation to its posterity, world without end! . . .

The late Mr. David Hume, in his posthumous works [*Dialogues Concerning Natural Religion*], places the powers of generation much above those of our boasted reason; and adds, that reason can only make a machine, as a clock or a ship, but the power of generation makes the maker of the machine. . . . he concludes that the world itself might have been generated, rather than created; that is, it might have been gradually produced from very small beginnings, increasing by the activity of its inherent principles, rather than by a sudden evolution [the word meant "preformation" to orthodox thinkers of the time] of the whole by the Almighty fiat.—What a magnificent idea of the infinite power of the Great Architect! The Cause of Causes! Parent of Parents! Ens Entinum![17]

Finally, Darwin's materialism implies not only the self-sufficiency of matter but also its indestructibility—what he calls "world without end." This notion was an explicit and major point in the materialism of the classical atomists.[18] The following beautifully written note in Darwin's *The Temple of Nature* suggests a final conflagration, as in Heraclitus; but in Darwin's conflagration matter is not destroyed but only reshuffled, and evolution begun again:

hence the quantity or number of organized bodies, and their improvement in size, as well as their happiness, has been continually increasing, . . . and will probably continue to increase till the whole terraqueous sphere, and all that inhabit it, shall dissolve by a general conflagration, and be again reduced to their elements.

  Thus all the suns, and the planets which circle round them, may again sink into one central chaos; and may again, by explosions, produce a new world; which, in process of time, may resemble the present one, and at length again undergo the same catastrophe! These great events may be the result of the immutable laws impressed on matter by the Great Cause of Causes, Parent of Parents, Ens Entinum![19]

Darwin ends this speculation, like his previous ones, with a reference to a divine creator; and his doing so suggests a major difficulty in reading the eighteenth-century *philosophes:* their ambivalence with regard to Deism. Most of them, like Darwin, retain vestiges of the argument from design—that the mechanical perfectness of nature implies the existence of a master mechanic creator. But, as the speculations about forces in matter became more and more evolutionary, or generative, the argument from design became more and more of a vestigial appendage. For example, when Darwin borrows Hume's phrase that the world might have been generated rather than created, the function of the first cause has shrunk from the devising of an intricate Newtonian world machine to the squirting out of the first DNA molecule. When Darwin argues that matter is indestructible, the corollary is that it was not created, and the first cause has disappeared altogether. In any case, the more orthodox Deists sensed rightly that the speculations of Darwin, as well as of Hume, were dangerous. The most eloquent late statement of the argument from design, William Paley's *Natural Theology* (1802), was said to have been written to refute Darwin's *Zoonomia.*[20]

  The deists should have been frightened by Darwin, and he himself should have been frightened because the implications of his imaginative world view, as well as those of Lockean analysis, which he understood, were terrifying. In his first published prose, a paper

read to the Royal Society in 1757, Darwin is caustically aware of
the prevalence of error even in a rigorously analytic method:

> Every theoretical inquiry, whose basis does not rest upon experiments,
> is at once exploded in this well-thinking age; where truth, under your pa-
> tronage, has at length broke thro' those clouds, with which superstition,
> policy, or parade, had overwhelmed her. But experiments themselves,
> gentlemen, are not exempted from fallacy. A strong inventive faculty, a
> fine mechanic hand, a clear unbiassed judgment, are at once required
> for the contrivance, conduct, and application, of experiments; and even
> where these are joined (such is the condition of humanity!) error too
> frequently intrudes herself, and spoils the work.[21]

If we add to this personal skepticism the implications of Lockean
epistemology—that all we can know are visual images which themselves are only general approximations—the conclusion suggests
that man is a blind blunderer stumbling about, to borrow William
Wordsworth's phrase, in worlds not realized.[22]

In addition, the cosmogony that the *philosophes* thought they must
hypothesize was consistent with this skeptical epistemology because
it posited a world of infinite possibility and of continuous movement.
The notion of perfectibility, which is usually associated with Darwin
as well as with William Godwin and other radical thinkers, is
deceiving here. They believed less in perfectibility as leading to
something perfect or even "better" than in malleability or simply
change.[23] And this uncompromising vision, or hypothesis, of
change, which reappeared in the eighteenth century with the French
philosophes and which is eloquently present in Darwin, was stubbornly materialistic. And materialism, like Lockean epistemology,
in its most rigorous form finally gives way to skepticism.[24] Hence
the end result of the imaginative speculation of the *philosophes* can
be summed up in the words of Aristophanes, "Whirl is king,
having deposed Zeus."[25] Even more terrifying, however, is the
conclusion of Hume that we cannot even be sure of skepticism.

II *Double Truth and the Comic Vision*

In spite of all this skepticism, the *philosophes* were a merry lot
who seemed actually to be liberated by their speculative vision.
La Mettrie is said to have been a jolly prankster, and he died from
gourmandizing. Diderot was a notorious bon vivant, while David
Hume was reputed to have been a serene and joyous liver.[26] The

morose livers and those who could not appreciate the jokes of life in the eighteenth century seem to have been more common among the orthodox.[27] Darwin himself led an exuberant, joyous, and even sensuous life which Hesketh Pearson describes well in his biography.[28] But Darwin refuses even in his speculative writing to acknowledge the awesome and dehumanizing terror implied by his conclusions. In fact, his theories include wonderful arguments to support the notion that the sum of animal pleasure is always increasing as the whirl of matter moves on. For example, he theorizes that sexual reproduction succeeded asexual reproduction partially in order to produce more pleasure.[29] The following quotation not only anticipates notions of psychosomatic illness but also illustrates Darwin's theoretical search for pleasure:

> Besides the pleasure, which attends the irritations produced by the objects of lust and hunger, there seems to be a sum of pleasurable affection accompanying the various secretions of the numerous glands, which constitutes the pleasure of life, in contradistinction to the tedium vitae. This quantity or sum of pleasurable affection seems to contribute to the due or energetic performance of the whole moveable system, as well that of the heart and arteries, as of digestion and of absorption; since without the due quantity of pleasurable sensation, flatulency and hypochrondriacism affect the intestines, and a languor seizes the arterial pulsations and secretions, as occurs in great and continued anxiety of the mind.[30]

The implications of being liberated from the ghosts of a closed world into the random movement of a universe stretching infinitely over time and space would have been (and were, of course) disruptive to the social stability of eighteenth-century Europe. Even Darwin's simple description of body pleasure quoted above would have been disruptive to the puritanical sense of depravity. But only a limited number of readers could see the hidden implications in the radical speculative thinking of the time; for the rest, most of the implications were disguised with humor, with myths, and with frequent expressions of gratitude to God, "the Parent of Parents." This disguise of radical implications behind pious or flippant expression, which has been labeled the double-truth doctrine by modern scholarship, was practiced by the most radical thinkers, including La Mettrie, as well as by more orthodox theologians.[31] The orthodox arguments of Bishop Warburton, for example, that ancient myths could conceal hidden meanings that were not meant for the masses actually helped the radicals because it opened up literary devices that could be read piously but that also could express speculative materialism.[32] In an important article, Irwin Primer has recently shown that Darwin used the double-truth doctrine at least in *The Temple of Nature,* his last poem:

> Darwin's use of ambiguity as a protective screen is easily seen in his references to God. Does this poem advocate a belief in God? Yes or no, we reply, depending upon what one makes of Darwin's affinities with Hartley and Priestley, and of the charges of materialism levelled against all three. Darwin carefully avoids any overt implications of irreligion, atheism, blasphemy and the like. . . . But much more striking is Darwin's subordination of biblical to pagan allusions. The Christian myth, in his hands, is no better than any other; all are treated as vessels of truth. By such means many a radical deist in the eighteenth century disguised his departure from Christian faith.[33]

The point of disguising radical speculation behind the double-truth doctrine was in part expediency, as in the case of Buffon who piously repudiates his theories of vast geological time (while keeping the evidence in) so that he could continue to publish the *Histoire naturelle.* The *philosophes* had much to fear, for in France, there was the official censor; and, even in England, government pamphleteering bore down heavily on "radicals." Professor Primer shows convincingly that Darwin was under attack from the *Anti-Jacobin* as well as from other organs of the conservative reaction that swept England in the 1790's.[34] But Darwin was actually practicing disguise and a kind of ambivalence toward his most radical speculation even in the earliest of his major works, "The Loves of the Plants" (1789). In fact, the best way to understand the double-truth doctrine in Darwin (possibly also in other of the *philosophes)* is to see it not only as expediency but also as a profound part of an overall vision. In order to go as far with his materialistic speculations as he did, Darwin had to disguise the implications even from himself. He had to erect a defense against the terrifying conclusions that he was approaching.

Darwin's psychological defenses and the literary devices that he uses to implement them constitute his comic vision. This comic tone or attitude that runs through all of Darwin's writings can be illustrated by his treatment of two images or themes: the notion of love and marriage and the image of circular movement. Geoffrey Hartman has recently written that Wordsworth's epistemology is a "love-epistemology,"[35] and he means that Wordsworth has the power of generating enough confidence in his own personal identity so that he is able "to know" the external world completely the way a totally self-confident lover is able to know any woman. In other words, Hartman offers new terminology to explain the two-fold way by which Wordsworth is able to solve the epistemological problem raised by the Lockean method: Wordsworth knows himself completely and hence can know the external world completely through love.

Hartman's terminology is useful, for it might be said that Darwin, who had not discovered Wordsworth's source of confidence, has a "marriage-epistemology" based on the comic acceptance of the limits to true love. The various limits on love are both physical and psychological, but all of them center around one dilemma: that a strongly developed personal identity is needed in order to give love, while, at the same time, this identity would have to be obliterated in any total union with "the other." Such limits are obvious and logical so that, if the love metaphor is used consistently for epistemology, the limits become apparent and the "total knowing" must degenerate into a marriage compromise in which the limits on love are accepted and made the best of. In other words, any treatment of erotic or sexual happiness, of which there is a great deal in Darwin, represents an acceptance of the marriage compromise, an acceptance of limited love that must end rather than a quixotic pursuit of unlimited love. Darwin, I think, insists on the logical use of the love metaphor; hence, he concludes in emphasizing marriage compromise and erotic love, whereas Wordsworth, like most of the Romantics, keeps "loving" and "knowing" in a blindly assertive and illogical way.

Elizabeth Sewell, one of the more sympathetic readers of Darwin in recent times, has pointed out Darwin's preoccupation with sex in conjunction with the Orpheus myth in his writing:

> It is this [plant sexuality] in Linnaeus which Darwin primarily celebrates, moving on from there to celebrate sex itself in *Phytologia* [a prose treatise on plant life] as "the chef d'oeuvre," the masterpiece of nature.
>
> The Orphic mind is active at this point, and we begin to see what lies behind the shift in our prevailing Orpheus figure from that of the ordering of nature to that of the search for Eurydice.[36]

But Miss Sewell fails to emphasize one aspect of the myth: the impossibility of any complete and final consummation in the love;

therefore, she does not completely understand Darwin's comic vision. It is implicit in the story of Orpheus that love and marriage cannot achieve the union that human beings would like. The comic vision expresses full awareness of this limitation and attempts to make the best of it. In fact, comic writers traditionally have used marriage contracts as symbols for a more general compromise with, or understanding of, the imperfect aspects of the human condition and an important part of the overall effect of Darwin's poems is his comic vision as it is expressed in part through the marriage theme.

Another image that illustrates Darwin's comic vision is the image of circles. Many circles are referred to in his verse; but, more importantly, the poems themselves embody eccentricity in the literal sense: centrifugal movement in all directions, continual playing on the periphery of experience.[37] There are focal points, or organizing principles, in the plot structure of the poems: the speeches of the Goddess in *The Botanic Garden* and the tour through the Temple of Nature in the poem of that name. And there are transitional devices pulling the edges toward the center: primarily the principle of contrast. But the movement in each of the poems is at least centrifugal: toward the notes at the bottom of the page, toward the additional notes at the end of each volume, and toward all topics imaginable.

The least centrifugal of the three poems is *The Temple of Nature*: it has a more highly developed frame story and setting in the tour through the Temple; it has fewer Homeric similes, fewer plot incidents; and the organization appears to be simpler. But, even though it is not quite so lush and various as the two earlier poems, *The Temple of Nature* is by no means simple in its plot. The poem does have the advantage of expressing more clearly and more abstractly Darwin's recurrent themes. In the third canto of this poem, in which the priestess of Nature explains man's psychology, Darwin includes some images that seem to represent the whirling circles of his plots in which the details on the circumferences, like the planets and the sun, are moving in several circles at once:

> The Giant Form on Nature's centre stands,
> And waves in ether his unnumber'd hands;
> Whirls the bright planets in their silver spheres,
> And the vast sun round other systems steers.[38]

In Darwin's plots, as in the universe, there is no one center. Or rather, if there is one (and the above passage, of course, says there is), it cannot be found. What is important are the various circumferences; and in Darwin's plots, just as in the universe, they are "unnumber'd."

The fact that Darwin's literary strategy has committed him to playing continually on the circumference, while, at the same time, he realizes that there must be a center, helps to produce his ironic detachment or his comic tone. Other, more important, devices also create this tone, as I show later; but the plot strategy is possibly the reason for it—or more precisely, a symptom of the reason for it. Darwin chooses to play at the periphery, to explore the great variety of the circumference; but he longs for the center. We might infer that Darwin wanted his plots diffuse or that he wanted continual imaginative speculation instead of certainty. However, he is resigned to these limitations because he cannot have it any other way: he is committed to the infinite variety of things (from shooting stars to electric eels) and wants them all in his poems; and the very nature of this situation is that he then cannot have only one thing. Thus, he chooses the infinite variety of things, the materialism of the *philosophes,* over the unity of some belief; and the result is a rich mélange that holds the potential for a high comic tone of acceptance of limitation.

This combination of an expanding sense of potential with the comic acceptance of limitation can also be seen in Darwin's personality. The man seems to have been as eccentric as his plots and as sadly aware of limitation. A few comments from his friend and first biographer, Anna Seward, about his personality are particularly provocative:

Conscious of great native elevation above the general standard of intellect, he became, early in life, sore upon opposition, whether in argument or conduct, and always, revenged it by sarcasm of very keen edge. . . . Perhaps this proneness to suspicion mingled too much of art in his wisdom. . . .

Though Dr. Darwin's hesitation in speaking precluded his flow of colloquial eloquence, it did not impede, or at all lessen, the force of that conciser quality, *wit.* Of satiric wit he possessed a very peculiar species.[39]

Like his plots, Darwin seems to have tried to do so much that he was continually in danger of collapse; but he would not settle for less. His stammer, his caustic sarcasm, and his deliberate artificiality of manner were all signs of what Elizabeth Schneider describes so well in Coleridge as the conflict between the awareness of exceptional powers and the awareness of impotence.[40] This psychological dilemma is similar to that of the expanding circle doomed to collapse because of its very expansion.

Perhaps here is the point at which to consider the weakness of Darwin's literary strategy, the outgrowth of his comic, materialist vision. Few people enjoy the centrifugal diffuseness of nature, for they long for the unifying focal points of belief that Darwin cannot emphasize. Similarly, few people enjoy the artificial language that is meant to express comic defense; they prefer the illusion of simplicity. Darwin chose both artifice of verse form and diffuseness of plotting. Oliver Elton correctly calls the plotting of his works Darwin's most fatal defect: "it is simply that he finds nothing irrelevant to his topic."[41] Dr. Beddoes, Darwin's most faithful imitator, contracted a case of this same fatal exuberance;[42] for the following modern description of Beddoes' poem *Alexander's Expedition* (1792), which could be a description of any of Darwin's cantos, explains why Beddoes, like Darwin, is no longer widely read:

> The poem itself is no more than 562 lines, and the rest of the book is taken up by the Advertisement, Notes and Observations. The range of the author's learning is impressive, and his style stimulating. It is spirited and cursory, touching on every subject, lingering on none. The Advertisement deals with poetry and philosophy, with education and the structure of society, and we get the impression that the author with a few strokes of his pen is going to expound the entire universe. . . . The notes to his own poem are longer than the narrative. They comprise history and fable, geography and climate, vegetation, architecture and politics.[43]

Thus, Darwin's restless, centrifugal energy attracted an imitator who wrote almost equally diffuse and splintered plots. The poems also attracted the imitation of parody in the anonymous "The Loves of the Triangles." But, in a sense, there was no need for the parody because Darwin's literary strategy parodies itself. And here we see the difficulty of disliking his weakness: it is also the source of great fun. Furthermore, this weakness communicates the notion of comic limitation because, while it continually promises "to expound the entire universe," this can never be done with centrifugal movement; for spiraling movement only produces more periphery surface to expound. Thus, absurdity, comic acceptance, and even the pathos of the pratfall are all communicated in the assumptions underlying such a literary strategy. No scientist, or curiosity seeker, or *philosophe,* or lover of life's variety can deny the fascination of everything on the periphery of experience in favor of the unity of the center. Every life force pulls him away from the center and toward spiraling digression and disintegration. But, at the same time, every demand of rhetoric and of common sense insists that he bend experience around some unifying topic or center, which possibly may be only the absurdity of death itself. The resulting tension produces the comic literary effect of compromise of the recognition of limitation.

In a sense, Darwin compromises because he refuses to confront the absurdity of a materialistic world in which every event is unique. So as a defense he draws a circle of words and myths around this dumb center of absurdity. And the fact that such a center can have no meaning at all makes the circle of words all the more important. The fact that love can never be enough makes the marriage-compromise all the more important. Darwin's comic vision is communicated (although it has not been well understood) by means of his extremely artificial and intricate use of myths and words—his marriage-compromise with language.

III *Myth and Artifice as Necessary Ornamentation*

Darwin uses myth consciously as allegory for his scientific theories; and, since his scientific theories were not mechanistic and fixed ones, he uses a number of myths variously, sometimes facetiously, and in shotgun fashion. A perceptive critic, Robert Scholes, writing recently on literary theory, describes this use of myth, although he is applying it to modern novelists, notably to John Barth:

All symbols become allegorical to the extent that we understand them. Thus the really perceptive writer is not merely conscious that he is using mythic materials: He is conscious that he is using them consciously. He *knows,* finally, that he is allegorizing. Such a writer, aware of the nature of categories, is not likely to believe that his own mythic lenses really capture the truth. Thus his use of myth will inevitably partake of the comic. . . . He knows too much—that is the modern writer's predicament, and that is precisely what prevents his perspective from being seriously mythic.[44]

Darwin definitely knows too much; but, unlike the Romantics, he does not try to escape into an unknown center of absurdity. He does not let the death wish dominate him; he opts for life. He stays gleefully on the surface with his knowledge.

In the use of myth, Darwin is almost pragmatic. He uses whatever he thinks will create a provocative analogy, and he is not troubled with trying to discover one central myth—not troubled because he basically understands, I think, that there is no such final unity. But, rather than submit completely to materialistic flux, he uses the suggestiveness of myth for what it is worth. The fact that myth is not worth a great deal to him is an indication of his intellectual honesty; the fact that he uses this imperfect tool is an indication of his humanness. He says pragmatically that "since natural objects are allied to each other by many affinities, every kind of theoretic distribution of them adds to our knowledge by developing some of their analogies."[45]

Darwin makes numerous comments about his use of stories from Classical mythology. In the poems, many of these comments appear in the notes that explain to the reader why a particular story is being versed. For example, the following note is attached to a version of the Adonis myth in *The Temple of Nature*:

The Egyptian figure of Venus rising from the sea seems to have represented the Beauty of organic Nature; which the philosophers of that country, the magi, appear to have discovered to have been elevated by earthquakes from the primeval ocean. But the hieroglyphic figure of Adonis seems to have signified the spirit of animation or life, which was perpetually wooed or courted by organic matter, and which perished and revived alternately. Afterwards the fable of Adonis seems to have given origin to the first religion promising a ressurection from the dead . . . .[46]

Earlier in the same poem Darwin explains that his allusions to various myths are "scenical representations" of knowledge. But, like the visual images in Lockean psychology, these stories can only be arbitrary counters to push around arbitrarily. Even though he does place great emphasis on his "scenical representations," especially in *The Temple of Nature*, as Irwin Primer argues, Darwin is very much aware of the basic limitations inherent in these emblems and is in a sense continually mocking his own serious use of myth. For example, in the "proem" addressed to the "Gentle Reader" of his earliest long poem "The Loves of the Plants" he writes: "Lo, here a Camera Obscura is presented to thy view, in which are lights and shades dancing on a whited canvas, and magnified into

apparent life!—if thou art perfectly at leisure for such trivial amusement, walk in, and view the wonders of my Inchanted Garden."[47]
He believes in his art, he believes in myth, and he believes in their
serious power to reveal a certain amount of truth; but, at the
same time, he does not believe.

If the thick texture of myth is an imperfect tool that Darwin
uses comically because he must use some tool, then his use of words
themselves is similar. The basic inability of all language to center
in finally on any subject, which is the heritage of Locke, is the starting
point for understanding Darwin's use of language. To compensate
for this limitation, Darwin thickens language and gleefully uses
all the artificiality he can muster. In other words, he turns the
liability into an asset—the comic reaction to any liability. This
chapter is not the place to describe all of his many language devices,
but they include intricacies of rhetoric and diction, as well as a
rather skillful use of the fixed prosody of the heroic couplet.[48]
To appreciate Darwin's poems in particular, the reader needs to
know a little bit about his word devices; more importantly, the
reader needs to learn to delight in the intricacies of words for their
own sake. For this sophisticated use of words, words, words is a
major element in Darwin's comic vision.

Darwin received the Classical education that taught, and he was
continually exposed to the Augustan literature that celebrated,
what W.K.Wimsatt, Jr., has named, with regard to Alexander Pope,
"an antique kind of respect for the word."[49] Darwin was educated
at Chesterfield School and St. John's College, Cambridge (Wordsworth's college), before studying medicine. Throughout his years
in school he wrote verses, as Charles Darwin attests in quoting a
letter written by Erasmus at the age of sixteen to his sister Susannah:
"was I to give you a journal of a Week, it would be stuft [*sic*] so full
of Greek and Latin as translation, verses, themes annotation Exer-
cises and ye like it would not only be very tedious and insipid but
perfectly unintelligible to any but Schoolboys."[50] When Darwin
began to write his major poems, he chose to use all of the verbal
and rhetorical complexity of the Augustan literature, thus asserting
this "respect for the word."

This attitude (the conservative Augustan delight in artifice)
is particularly appropriate to the comic acceptance of the Lockean
dilemma that words can never have an exact one-to-one relationship with things, but that they are our only means of communicating

about things, because words themselves become the prime focus of attention. Since even simple words (and images) are only abstractions from things, it would be fruitless for a writer to try to use nonartificial words that have a direct connection with what they signify. The only connections possible are the abstracted connections among words, and presumably the more complex connections are capable of symbolizing more relationships with the external world. In other words, Darwin's artifice, an attempt to thicken the relationships among words, is a way of increasing the meaning of words and, at the same time, of expressing the limitations of words.

For example, meter, as distinct from rhythm, is one of the more artificial attributes of language; and, when a writer chooses to verse his thoughts, to put them into a metrical pattern, he chooses to focus attention on something purely verbal and abstract. Thus, in a poem describing a beautiful woman the imagery may appear to be beautiful and sensuous, just as the woman is beautiful or sensuous; but the meter, if the poem is metrical, is less likely to appear directly similar to something about the woman. Of course, nothing in the poem, neither the images, nor the metrics, nor the punctuation is actually anything other than language; but, if the writer wants to emphasize the difference between the words and the woman, one way to do so is to make the words strictly metrical. No woman is metrical, although some may be rhythmic.

Darwin's comic tone and his characteristic use of thick language stress the fact that the actual woman is always out of reach. He always uses meter, a limitation; but, when the intricacies of the language dance around the actual woman, and the dance itself is a partial compensation for the loss of the woman, a liability is made an asset. Darwin especially likes the figures of speech involving the arrangement of words, the rhetorical schemes of parallelism and repetition, and especially reverse parallelism or chiasmus. Although I make a close analysis in later chapters of many passages, it is useful now to describe in detail Darwin's use of the figure of chiasmus in order to illustrate his thickly textured use of words.

The fugure of chiasmus is any balanced parallelism in which the elements of the two halves mirror each other, or are reversed. The figure is traditionally used to gain variety in balance or to provide a rhyme word. But chiasmus also may serve a purpose other than that of achieving variety. It gives the impression of circular motion; it is a way of expressing, in sheer, formal, geometric relationships, what Primer calls, in discussing Darwin's use of myth, "the eternal return."[51] In a book on the circle in literature, Georges Poulet also suggests that the smaller elements of verbal style can express circularity: "In certain schiastic [*sic*] passages of Saint Augustine, one can see a verbal representation of the circular movement by which the Son is found in the Father, and the Father in the Son: "'*In pricipio erat verbum, et verbum erat apud Deum, erat verbum.*' These variations on the famous passage of the Gospel according to Saint John, have no other purpose than to form a circle of words equivalent to the spiritual circle constituted by the Trinity."[52]

Darwin is fascinated by chiasmus, and he writes crossing or chiastic lines again and again regardless of what he is describing. The complexity of the elements reversed or mirrored also varies from simple chiasmus in one line to very intricate arrangements. In the following example, the repeated word at each end of the line and the alliteration of the other element makes the chiastic return simple and obvious:

> Two *brother swains, of Collin's gentle name,*
> *The same their features, and their forms the same.*[53]

Darwin often uses a verb at each end of the line with the substantives of the verbs as the middle elements; and, in the following example, alliteration also underlines the chiastic return:

> *Sudden with rage their injur'd bosoms burn,*
> *Retort the insult, or the wound return.*[54]

More often than not, chiasmus occurs in the second line of a couplet; but Darwin also places it in the first line, as in the following description of the moon:

> *Dimpled with vales, with shining hills emboss'd,*
> *And roll'd round Earth her airless realms of frost.*[55]

Or he uses it in both lines of a couplet, as in the following example in which the Botanic Goddess is speaking to the gnomes of earth:

> *Climb the rude steeps, the granite-cliffs surround,*
> *Pierce with steel points, with wooden wedges wound.*[56]

Or he uses it to link two couplets by placing it in the second line

of one and in the first line of the next, as in the following example
in which the Botanic Goddess describes how "sympathy" should
behave:

> *To friendless Virtue, gasping on the strand,*
> *Bare her warm-heart, her virgin arms expand,*
> *Charm with kind looks, with tender accents cheer,*
> *And pour the sweet consolatory tear.*[57]

Occasionally, Darwin writes a verse paragraph that includes five
or six chiastic lines, a greater concentration of them than is usual
in the couplet. One example of these is appropriate to quote because
it is a description of the invention of paper and of its artful use.
The following passage actually describes three applications of paper
for the alphabet, for mathematics, and for music:

> *Till to astonish'd realms* PAPYRA *taught*
> *To paint in mystic colours Sound and Thought.*
> *With Wisdom's voice to print the page sublime,*
> *And mark in adament the steps of Time,*
> *—Three favour'd youths her soft attention share,*
> *The fond disciples of the studious Fair,*
> * *Hear her sweet voice, the golden process prove;*
> * *Gaze, as they learn; and, as they listen, love.*
> *The first from Alpha to Omega joins*
> *The letter'd tribes along the level lines;*
> *Weighs with nice ear the vowel, liquid, surd,*
> *And breaks in syllables the volant word.*
> *Then forms the next upon the marshal'd plain*
> *In deepening ranks his dexterous cypher-train;*
> *And counts, as wheel the decimating bands,*
> * *The dews of Aegypt, or Arabia's sands,*
> *And then the third on four concordant lines*
> * *Prints the lone crotchet, and the quaver joins;*
> * *Marks the gay trill, the solemn pause inscribes,*
> *And parts with bars the undulating tribes.*
> *Pleased round her cane-wove throne, the applauding crowd*
> * *Clapp'd their rude hands, their swarthy foreheads bow'd;*
> *With laud acclaim "a present God!" they cry'd,*
> *"A present God!" rebellowing shores reply'd.*[58]

The asterisks mark the six lines that are chiastic. In addition, the
second and third lines of the quotation constitute a more complicated kind of chiastic arrangement in which the adverbial ideas

modifying the two infinitives are in a "crossing" position—one
after its infinitive; the next, before. In any case, for a description
of artifice in language, numbers, and music Darwin uses a fair
preponderance of one of his more artificial figures.

He also writes more complicated chiastic arrangements than the
relatively simple one of phrases with parallel meaning and with
the verb at each end. In the following two examples, the meaning
is not parallel but is nearly antithetical, and the verbs are not at the
end:

> —*High o'er the chequer'd vault with transient glow*
> *Bright lustres dart, as dash the waves below.*[59]

> *New woods aspiring clothe their hills with green,*
> *Smooth slope the lawns, the grey rock peeps between.*[60]

In the first example, the verbs do have parallel meaning; but the
substantives are at opposite extremes, sky-lights and waves; and
the chiasmus is not bounded by the verbs although alliteration
does underline the mirroring effect. In the second example, later
in the same description of the gardens of the Duke of Devonshire,
Darwin writes an equally complex chiasmus in which each half
includes three elements with the verbs in the middle and adverbs
at each end.

In addition to chiasmus in which the two halves are placed in
succeeding half-lines, Darwin also writes patterns in which the
two halves occur elsewhere in the couplet. In these complex arrangements, there is also generally straight parallelism between the two
lines of the couplet. In other words, in places Darwin sets up a
tension between inverted order, or circular patterns, and straight
parallelism, or linear patterns. For example, we have the description of a nursing baby:

> *No voice so sweet attunes his cares to rest,*
> *So soft no pillow, as His Mother's breast!*[61]

This intricate pattern of inversion, combined with straight parallelism, is quite common in his last poem *The Temple of Nature,*
especially in Darwin's description of birth, growth, and death.
For instance, in his account of the transformation of water animals
into land animals, there is a couplet in which the two lines are perfectly parallel in syntax and sense except that there is chiastic inversion of the adjectives and nouns in each line:

> *Cold gills aquatic form respiring lungs,*
> *And sounds aerial flow from slimy tongues.*[62]

Furthermore, the first element of the couplet, "cold gills," seems to go with the last element, "slimy tongues," while the two substantives in the middle also go together. Thus, the arrangement appears to be perfectly parallel; but it also includes circular, back and forth, movement.

The best example of this tension between linear parallelism and circular chiasmus occurs in a couplet dealing with the opposition between life and death:

> *Organic forms with chemic changes strive,*
> *Live but to die, and die but to survive.*[63]

In addition to the straight parallelism of the first line, the alternation in the second line of finite verb, infinitive, finite verb, infinitive is linear; but the meaning, as well as the internal rhyme of "live" and "survive," is chiastic. At the same time, the two halves of the second line express the antithetical relationship of life and death, although the chiasmus makes it seem more like paradox than in any of the previous examples. But, by constructing chiasmus with the hint of linear parallelism, Darwin avoids a complete surrender to paradox and retains a greater, more interesting complexity.

To suggest that a rhetorical figure such as chiasmus can have expressive potentialities beyond its function of providing artful variety in the stringing together of parallel words or ideas is to suggest a dimension of "the word" that is highly subtle and intellectualized. In fact, Anna Seward concludes that the primary appeal of Darwin's verse was not to emotion but to intellect. She does not mention the figures of speech, such as chiasmus, probably because these terms of rhetoric were second nature to them because they were associated with their earliest education. The use of such names in the analysis of the poetry of Pope, and now of Darwin, is actually the revival of an older terminology that the eighteenth-century writers themselves did not use.

Miss Seward does make a distinction, however, between verse that appeals to the emotions and verse that delights "the eye, the taste, and the fancy" in the following comment: "Dr. Darwin's excellence consists in delighting the eye, the taste, and the fancy, by the strength, distinctness, elegance, and perfect originality of his pictures; and in delighting the ear by the rich cadence of his numbers; but the passions are generally asleep, and seldom are the nerves thrilled by his imagery, impressive and beauteous as it is, or by his landscapes, with all their vividness."[64]

The comic and highly intellectual acceptance of the limitations of language is also in part the reason for Darwin's gaudy visual images to which Miss Seward refers. Given his basic skepticism, he builds a richly sensuous world of proliferating visual images that is not the real world, but it is as sensuous as the real world seems to be. Darwin undoubtedly liked the verse form of the heroic couplet partly because the sound patterns, such as chiasmus, could be represented so well visually on the page and could thus complement his more obvious visual imagery.

In conjunction with visual detail, another device is worked over and over again by Darwin and becomes a characteristic of his comic style and tone. This device is what criticism has labeled "eighteenth-century poetic diction," and what is generally meant are two-word epithets that are periphrastic, such as "feathery people" for birds.[65] In view of Darwin's other stylistic devices, we would expect him to make as full use as he could of this additional device for thickening language and adding to visual imagery. A typical passage is the following account from *The Temple of Nature* of the way in which the fish and birds, two favorite classes for periphrases, respond happily to the appearance of sexual love. Darwin uses a conventional periphrasis for each group of animals, as well as other two-word groups that resemble conventional poetic diction but are less common and probably his own creation, such as "slimy foreheads." One effect is the accumulation of an almost excessive amount of accurate visual detail ranging from the scales to the slime to the wings and back to the water:

> *Pleased as they [the lovers] pass along the breezy shore*
> *In twinkling shoals the scaly realms adore,*
> *Move on quick fin with undulating train,*
> *Or lift their slimy foreheads from the main.*
> *High o'er their heads on pinions broad display'd*
> *The feather'd nations shed a floating shade.*[66]

An important use of poetic diction and even visual detail in Darwin's verse is to control tone or, rather, to help create his mixed, comic tone. Most interpreters of poetic diction in the eighteenth century have observed that a set of conventional terms helps to emphasize any variation from or new combination of them.

C. V. Deane even hints that poetic diction became a comic tool of self-parody at the same time that it was still being used seriously: "the authors of phrases of this type [poetic diction] not only show a connoisseur's relish in the amenities of a settled style; they illuminate the object from a fresh angle by revealing its unconscious humour."[67] Darwin not only uses occasional variations from the conventional formulas for comic purposes but also continually overloads his conventional descriptions for a purpose other than sensuousness. Along with his celebration of the rich gaudiness of the physical world, there is an ever present twinkle of humor in his verse as he contemplates this or that natural object.

This mixed tone is undoubtedly in the tradition of the mock-heroic of the early part of the eighteenth century. Pope treated dangerous topics in a playful manner, but Darwin treats everyday things in an elevated, pompous manner with a humorous twinkle.[68] The effect, however, is similar: both writers are deeply concerned with big themes (Pope's are more social; Darwin's, scientific); but both realize that their audience, indeed their whole society, is trivial by comparison to their themes, and that no final answers are available. The sanity of much eighteenth-century literature can be seen in this sort of ironic detachment. Since nothing measures up to one's hopes, the only way to retain some hope is to erect an artificial defense. In literature, this defense can be erected with a thick, verbal texture and with a mixed tone. Darwin achieves this tone in various ways, but an example of how he does it with variations on the conventional poetic diction occurs in his description (already quoted in part above) of the advent of sexual love in nature. First the flowers learn to reproduce sexually, then the birds:

> Or buoy'd in air the plumy Lover springs,
> And seeks his panting bride on Hymen-wings.[69]

The phrase "plumy Lover" is a variation on the stock periphrasis "plumy kind" for birds.[70] A rather silly reduction of the elegant poetic diction to the level of eighteenth-century bedroom farce, the phrase is at the same time still within the basic pattern of the elevated diction, and thus the farce is partly serious.

Darwin continually achieves this mixed tone, however, with the whole complex of his elevated, sensuous, silly diction. The reader is continually shifting from laughter to awe—from admiring the silliness in the overblown description of an object to admiring the rich sensuousness with which the object is captured in the same description. The most notorious example of Darwin's refusal to call a spade a spade, which I have seen quoted in two discussions of poetic diction and attributed to Darwin in one of them, is the following couplet:

> *Metallic blade wedded to ligneous rod,*
> *Wherewith the rustic swain upturns the sod.*[71]

Spades, like all objects, are exactly this important; and yet in any "civilized" society, with other interests than the basic, elemental forces of nature (which cannot be known directly anyway), to call a spade a spade would be both impossible and disruptive.

Darwin's poetry, then, never tries to call a spade a spade any more than it tries to describe the actual rhythmic woman in metered language. Instead, the poetry dances around all possibilities with its ornate style. In a sense, his is simply the ornate style of much eighteenth-century literature (what Coleridge called "Gaudyverse"). Given Darwin's materialistic vision, however, this ornateness takes on a new role: that of comic defense. A favorite of the *philosophes* was the encyclopedic naturalist, Buffon, whose famous maxim on style was a commonplace in the eighteenth century.[72] When Buffon argued the *le style est l'homme même*—style is the man— he was confident that the real inner man and his relation to nature could be manifested in well-ordered and well-elaborated forms.[73] For Darwin, style is the man as a kind of compensation for the loss of certitude. His prose style is a somewhat different matter from his thick, comic poetry, although similar tonal effects exist even in his prose. But, in his poetry, Darwin is preeminently the dancing stylist because he cannot be sure of anything.

The *philosophes* liberated thought, and this liberation for the most advanced of them meant the acceptance of uncertainty. With this acceptance came the comic abandon, the freedom of thought, that was both exhilarating and terrifying. Darwin's poetry and prose becomes more meaningful if it is read in the context of these radical ideas and this comic style. A cheerful materialist, he was daring in his speculations; but, he was also shrewd enough to protect his own humanness against the implications of materialism by means of humor.

CHAPTER 2

The Botanic Garden

THE single most dominant tone of Darwin's poetry is its sense of provisional playfulness. He was apparently not sure that his imagination, or anyone's, would reveal anything significant; but he had to try. This playfulness is, of course, his comic defense or the withholding of himself from a total commitment to what he sensed would be absurdity. This overall comic deviousness in Darwin's attitude governed the method of composition, the order of publication, and the ingredients of his first major literary production, *The Botanic Garden*. Anna Seward, who gave him the idea for the poem, had much to say in her book on Darwin about his skepticism and comic withdrawal, as I have already shown; but it is relevant to quote her most pithy statement about his comic refusal to place final confidence in anything: "Extreme was his scepticism to human truth. From that cause he often disregarded the accounts his patients gave of themselves. . . . [He had] an apparent want of confidence in mankind."[1]

Darwin's lack of confidence in mankind, in truth, and even in himself explains why he did not attempt any ambitious literary work until middle age, why he was continually devious about the purposes of his writings (especially his poetry), and why he even made one of his good friends, Miss Seward herself, a victim of plagiarism. (With regard to this last puzzling fact, it seems that Darwin would commit dishonest acts so long as they were not too dishonest; this characteristic is a comic, almost cynical, acceptance of limitation.) Also, nearly everything I say about the themes, for instance, in the poems finds contradiction in the poems themselves; for Darwin is tricky as a poet.

The idea for the two poems of *The Botanic Garden* began to grow in Darwin's mind about the year 1777, and Miss Seward reports that he worked on the poems for ten years from 1779 to 1789. The poems were initially inspired by some verses that Miss Seward had written when Darwin had shown her a new botanic garden he had bought about a mile from Lichfield in order to grow his own medicinal herbs.[2] He probably wrote "The Economy of Vegetation" first since it includes at the beginning of Canto I the nearly twenty couplets that originally had been written by Miss Seward.[3] In 1789, however, he published the second part of the poem first, "The Loves of the Plants"; and he did not publish the first part until nearly three years later. Ten years after that *The Temple of Nature* appeared posthumously. "The Loves of the Plants," which is much simpler in subject matter and structure than either "The Economy of Vegetation" or *The Temple of Nature*, is a catalogue of plant sexuality based roughly on the Linnaean system of classification by sexual parts; that is, plants are classified according to the number and nature of the male and female organs on each individual. Darwin personifies plants and simply recounts some ninety short anecdotes of comic love-marriage situations among various ones. Each of the other two poems deals with a much wider range of natural history and scientific theory, although there are also a few longer, more wide-ranging stories in "The Loves of the Plants." All three poems are about the same length, and, of course, in heroic couplets.

All these poems are long out of print, but the copies of the many late eighteenth-century and early nineteenth-century editions that I have seen are beautiful books. Along with the couplet verse, the books contain many "footnotes," as well as many pages for each poem of "Additional Notes," in prose printed at the back. Each poem has printed with it numerous illustrations, mostly charts and drawings of plants, although there are also a few drawings to illustrate the narrative events. Several of the engravings for the illustrations were done by William Blake.[4] In other words, Darwin's London publisher, Joseph Johnson, invested heavily to produce fine books. We can only hope that there soon can be facsimile editions of them.

I *Encyclopedic Plots*

Each of Darwin's three major poems ("The Loves of the Plants," "The Economy of Vegetation," and *The Temple of Nature*) has four cantos ranging in length from four hundred to six hundred lines apiece. Cantos II and IV of "The Economy of Vegetation" contain slightly over six hundred lines. The amount of paraphrasable material, however, in this relatively small amount of verse is enormous. Wordsworth's *Prelude*, by contrast, contains many more lines

of verse; but I believe it could be paraphrased more easily and quickly
than these three poems of Darwin's. His plot incidents nearly defy
summary since there are so many of them—a statement supported
by the fact that, among the writers in English who have done
lengthy commentaries on Darwin's poems, only Anna Seward has
written a minute plot summary. But even her summary becomes
general and skimming in places.[5] In order to illustrate the kind of
plot of these poems, a closer summary than has yet been written of
the incidents in one canto is helpful; and I have chosen for summary
the first canto of "The Economy of Vegetation" because its first
canto is typical of the entire poem, as well as the one that introduces
the machinery and setting of the poem.

The opening speaker of the poem is the "Genius" of that place, a
botanic garden outside Lichfield. Promising that his entire menagerie
of personified elements, plants, and animals will perform he invites
the reader of taste and virtue to enter the garden; but he commands
less endowed people to stay away. He does add, however, that if a
"hapless maid" should be with the reader, his garden is also a
suitable retreat for sad lovers. Then, after ordering the weather to
behave, he summons the Botanic Goddess.[6] Before she arrives,
however, Darwin (that is, the poet himself) interrupts briefly to
praise the Genius for preserving the garden in peace and truth and
also for keeping it beautiful (Darwin has told the reader in a note
that he himself owns this garden). Then the poet describes the
arrival of the Goddess, but neither this passage about the Goddess
nor any of the passages in *The Temple of Nature* about female
characters is equal in kind or quality to the invocation of Venus at
the beginning of Lucretius' *De Rerum Natura*. But the celebration
of life that permeates Darwin's poems, as well as his use of females
as representatives for nature, constitute parallels to Lucretius.
The more obvious parallel, of course, is Darwin's strong leaning
toward materialism, as described in Chapter 1 above.

To continue, the *Botanic Goddess* descends in a car decked with
flowers; and, when it sets down, she steps out on "pansied grounds"
(1.68). The reader is told that it is spring. Gathered to greet the
Goddess is a choir of birds organized by Spring herself, as well as
representatives from each of the four Rosicrucian elements: the
Gnomes frolic around her feet; Sylphs flutter around her head;
Nymphs emerge from the streams; and Salamanders appear from
the sunbeams around her head, although Darwin avoids the term

"Salamander" and calls the representatives of fire "Fiery Forms." When the Goddess summons the element of fire to form in review, representatives of the element come from all over the universe and gather expectantly in front of her. She tells them that they, "Nymphs of primeval Fire," were the original catalyst that stimulated nature to begin the evolution of a "living" world from "the rude abyss" (11. 97–102). Then she describes the creation of the astral universe as a kind of explosive event.

The machinery is now established for the remainder of this canto. The Goddess continues to speak directly to the Salamanders whom she soon begins to call Nymphs, and she reminds them what their various functions are in the creation. First of all, they are told that they control all movements of light in outer space from shooting stars to the sun. The reader may become confused when the Goddess enumerates many varieties of heavenly bodies in one breathless burst of balanced couplets. But Darwin, beginning to use an organizational principle of contrast (one which he employs more or less in all of his poems), has the Goddess abruptly switch from a description of celestial light to a consideration of the center of the earth. She tells the Nymphs that they are responsible for volcanic action from the Andes to Mount Etna, and here uses her first Homeric simile to tell the story of Venus descending into the armory of Mount Etna to keep Vulcan company. One point is that even in the infernal regions underground these Nymphs are beautiful.

Switching her attention back above ground again, but not as high as the heavens, the Goddess next reminds the Nymphs of their function as residual heat in the earth's atmosphere after dark. She illustrates with a reference to two contemporary experiments with phosphorescence. The Goddess only mentions them in passing, but a long note explains these experiments to the reader. Phosphorescence is also illustrated by the Goddess with a brief reference to the story of Memnon's lyre, which was said to play when the rising sun shone on it, and Darwin also includes a long note about this reference. Obviously, from the way in which the Goddess speaks to them, these Nymphs have the benefit of both a scientific and Classical education. Moving from the consideration of phosphorescence to swamp gas, the Goddess makes a transition into a treatment of the role of heat or light in animals. She mentions the common firefly, a more exotic "tropic Beetle," phosphorescent water insects, and a South American electric eel about which Darwin supplies fascinating experimental information in a note. The electric eel reminds the Goddess of the Bird of Jove which has lightning in his claws, and Darwin reminds the reader that this bird is represented on an antique gem in the collection of the Grand Duke of Florence.

The transition into the next topic is one of progression: from animals to primitive man. The Goddess reminds the Nymphs how they had taught primitive man to use fire. She calls this skill the first art and describes it as the ability to convert a dangerous phenomenon into something useful.[7] In short, the Nymphs taught man to "list the dread Destroyer on his side" (1. 216). This paradox is illustrated by comparison to the Medusa in Egyptian myth who was terrible and yet at the same time emblematic of divine wisdom. Again using a transition based on progression, or a kind of contrast, the Goddess moves from primitive man to a consideration of the sophisticated men of Darwin's own time, the scientists. She reminds the Nymphs that they help chemists in particular do their work, and she names the discoverer of the process for producing phosphorus. The man's name is Kunkel, or Kunckel, from Hamburg, and Darwin supplies the expected note. Leaving science for four lines, the Goddess is reminded by the highly flammable properties of phosphorus of some lovesick maiden wasting away "by self-consuming fire" (1.236). Gunpowder is the next topic, but the inclusion of an early chemist, Roger Bacon, actually classifies it as a continuation of the previous topic. After telling the Nymphs that they had taught Bacon what he knew about gunpowder, the Goddess gives a description of an exploding charge that resembles the earlier picture of the creation of the universe: "Runs the quick fire along the kindling train" (1. 246).

From this description of a destructive force associated with heat or fire, the Goddess moves to a description of a productive force— the steam engine. She mentions the inventor, Thomas Savery, describes the piston mechanism, and then depicts several applications of the engine: it provides power for water pumps, millstones, and machines for coining money. When the Goddess begins to prophesy the future uses of the steam engine, she foresees steamships, motor cars, and airplanes. Finally, a long Homeric simile recounting the labors of Hercules illustrates the power of the steam engine.

The next topic is electricity, and the Nymphs are told of the role they play in the various electrical experiments of Darwin's time. The Goddess tells them that they are responsible for controlling the attraction or repulsion of gold leaves in an experiment, the details of which are given in a note, as well as for controlling the reactions of a volunteer maiden who agrees to touch an electrified rod while standing on wax. In describing other experiments in giving people mild electrical shocks, the Goddess suggests that electricity may have something to do with the operation of nerves in animals. At least, she describes vividly the passage of a current through the nerves and compares it to lightning, while in a note Darwin speculates on the neurology. The topic of electricity allows the Goddess to voice a twelve-line tribute to a martyr to science, one Dr. Richman, who had been killed in 1763 while conducting Benjamin Franklin's experiment for collecting electricity from thunderclouds. Franklin's successful experiment is then mentioned and compared to the story of Cupid's stealing lightning bolts from Jove.

Returning to the role of heat in bodily functions, which had been touched upon in the middle of the section on electricity, the Goddess tells the Nymphs that they feed the very fires of life through the process of respiration. Then the Goddess compares oxygen, because of its heat-producing properties, to immortal love in the myth in which it bursts from the egg of night at the time of creation. These stories of love, generation, and birth of individuals and of the cosmos are favorites of the Goddess. Thus this last function of heat, oxygen, or immortal love is important enough to produce a kind of climax; and with it the Goddess stops her summary of the various roles played by the Nymphs. She looks over the legions gathered around her and then begins to command the Nymphs to action—to make war against "the Fiend of Frost" (1. 439) in order to inaugurate spring; and she apparently forgets that she had originally arrived in a springlike setting. In any case, the thought of chasing the wintry fiend north leads her to a Homeric simile about chasing a wounded whale north. When she turns back to the Nymphs, she orders them to initiate germination in plants by means of heat, electricity, and light. Darwin's speculations in a note about the differences among these three and their different functions in promoting plant growth are interesting, for he is close to an understanding of photosynthesis.[8]

As the Goddess thinks about the advent of spring, she gives a sweeping panoramic description of trees leafing out in Canada and compares the process to the property of certain invisible inks made from Zaffre (or impure cobalt oxide) to snap into vision when they are warmed. In a note, Darwin tells the reader how to make these inks.

Next, in contrast, the Goddess commands the Nymphs to leave a region and go north when the Dog Star of August, Sirius, threatens to scorch the vegetation. The danger of scorching is illustrated by a reference to the story of Jove's killing the Theban princess, Semele, with his divine body heat, "his blazing form" (1. 505). At such times, the Nymphs are told to journey to the polar regions where it is always twilight, to melt the ice there into large ice floes, and to blow these into tropic climates. The Goddess says that to do so is not so preposterous as it sounds since large monsoon winds do cool the tropics, and Darwin supports her with more data in the notes. Similarly, if the sun at summer solstice evaporates too much moisture from vegetation, the Nymphs are commanded to gather an electrical storm and water the flowers—a command illustrated by the well-read Goddess with a final long comparison from the Bible; for, when Elijah on Mount Carmel invoked both fire and rain from heaven to destroy an idolatrous altar and to water a thirsty people, he undoubtedly called forth a thunderstorm. With this last simile, the Goddess stops, and the Nymphs go to carry out her command. Their departure is described by the poet as a huge fireworks display.

It should not be necessary to paraphrase more of Darwin's cantos in order to illustrate that the plot of each one resembles the plot of an encyclopedia, but one without the benefit of the alphabet for organization. The reader probably notices, however, that there are the rudiments of rhetorical organization; for it would be fruitless to assume, I think, that Darwin was simply careless and could have had a tighter plot if he had worked harder on the poems. Anna Seward tells us that he worked hard indeed on these poems, "corrected and polished with such elaborate care."[9] She also pinpoints the major restraining principle of organization which Darwin seems to use consistently but which is nearly lost to sight amid the diffuseness of the poems—the principle of contrast. Miss Seward finds it here and there through "The Loves of the Plants," and I have shown how it is used fairly often to provide transitions in the canto just paraphrased. Miss Seward generalizes: "Attentive to diversify them [the plants] by the varieties of landscape, we [sic] generally find this Poet producing contrasted scenery by the introduction of flowers or plants which are indigenous to climates strikingly the reverse of each other."[10]

In spite of such generalizations, however, and no matter how carefully we analyze while looking for structure, we are finally left, I think, with the image of an unalphabetized encyclopedia to describe Darwin's organization and plotting. But there is one additional ordering principle that Darwin toyed with in his characteristic playful manner. In fact, this principle is the most ambitious of all—hence his comic, or double-truth, attitude.

II   *An Eleusinian Mystery Religion—Maybe*

In his important article, Irwin Primer argues that Darwin believed in the truth of myths enough to make them, especially the stories connected with the Greek Eleusinian mysteries, the serious subject of his last poem.[11] Darwin himself best explains what this specific subject matter is and how it can work in a piece of literature. He makes this explanation several times and not just in *The Temple of Nature*. Also, numerous times in the notes of all three poems he alludes generally to the notion of a mystery cult which possesses secret knowledge and which expresses it only to the initiated through secret pictorial hieroglyphics. These references lead me to believe that not only *The Temple of Nature*, as Professor Primer boldly states, but all of Darwin's long poems are constructed as "scenical representations," or symbols of secret knowledge, on the analogy of the Eleusinian mysteries.[12]

In the long prose note about the Portland vase to "The Economy of Vegetation," Darwin explains fully what he understands the "scenical representations" in the Eleusinian mysteries to have been. The note, an extended essay in art criticism, interprets the symbolism of the figures on the vase in much the same way that I propose to interpret the random stories in the poems. It is a carefully elaborated statement that the images on this vase—as well as images on other gems and medallions that fascinated him and appear often in his notes—are allegorical or symbolic. The concepts that are concretized on the vase are simple enough, just as the representations in the ancient mystery religion of Eleusis probably dealt with familiar patterns that have often been restated in various religions and philosophies. In other words, Darwin, like the scholarly syncretists such as Charles Dupuis or Jacob Bryant, believes in something like the uniformity of all religious concepts; and Darwin has reached back for an ancient and obscure religious practice to serve as the vehicle for his belief—at the same time that his comic tone withholds complete belief.

According to Darwin, one set of figures on the vase represents man's mortality: "This central figure then appears to me to be an hieroglyphic or Eleusinian emblem of *Mortal Life. . . .* "[13] But similar figures on the other side of the vase represent to Darwin immortality and, connected with recurring life, love:

On the other compartment of this celebrated vase is exhibited an emblem of immortality, the representation of which was well known to constitute a very principle part of the shews at the Eleusinian mysteries. . . .

There is yet another figure which is concerned in conducting the manes or ghost to the realms of Pluto, and this is *Love*. . . . The antient God of love was of much higher dignity than the modern Cupid. He was the first that came out of the great egg of night, (Hesiod. Theog. V. CXX. Bryant's Mythol. Vol. II. p. 348.) and is said to possess the keys of the sky, sea, and earth. As he therefore led the way into this life, he seems to constitute a proper emblem for leading the way to a future life. See Bacon's works. Vol. I. p. 568. and Vol. III. p. 582. Quarto edit.

The introduction of love into this part of the mysteries requires a little further explanation. The Psyche of the Egyptians was one of their most favourite emblems, and represented the soul, or a future life; it was originally no other than the aurelia, or butterfly, but in after times was represented by a lovely female child with the beautiful wings of that insect. The aurelia, after its first stage as an eruca or caterpillar, lies for a season in a manner dead, and is inclosed in a sort of coffin, in this state of darkness it remains all the winter, but at the return of spring it bursts its bonds and comes out with new life, and in the most beautiful attire. The Egyptians thought this a very proper picture of the soul of man, and of the immortality to which it aspired. But as this was all owing to divine Love, of which Eros was an emblem, we find this person frequently introduced as a concomitant of the soul in general or Psyche. (Bryant's Mythol. Vol. II. p. 386) Eros, or divine Love, is for the same reason a proper attendant on the manes or soul after death, and much contributes to tell the story, that is, to shew that a soul or manes is designed by the descending figure.[14]

This long quotation gives a taste of Darwin's almost childlike openness, one which looks forward to the Romantics, and of his belief in the possibilities of relating and interpreting symbolically the abundance of stories from myth. But, on the other hand, Darwin interprets one of the figures on the vase as emblematic of the secrecy which was an important part of the Eleusinian mysteries as he understood them and as a forerunner of his comic detachment. He reads this figure of the Hierophant as being both a hermaphrodite and a clever mystifier: "the figure at the bottom of the vase would seem to represent a *Priestess* or *Hierophant*, whose office it was to introduce the initiated, and point out to them, and explain the exhibitions in the mysteries, and to exclude the uninitiated, calling out to them, 'Far, far retire, ye profane!' and to guard the secret of the temple. Thus the introductory hymn sung by the hierophant, according to Eusebius, begins, 'I will declare a secret to the initiated, but let the doors be shut against the profane.'"[15]

An important element in Darwin's understanding of the Eleusinian mysteries is his belief—one which was current in the scholarship of his time but which modern archaeology has apparently proved wrong—that the secret knowledge of the mysteries was transmitted from Egypt.[16] Thus, his frequent mention in his prefaces and notes of the allegorical or symbolic meaning of Egyptian myths also constitutes an oblique reference to the mysteries. For example, in the prefatory "apology" to "The Economy of Vegetation," Darwin does not mention the mysteries by name; but he does express a belief in the communicative power of "hieroglyphic" stories that is consistent with his note on the Portland vase and with his other references to the mysteries:

Many of the important operations of Nature were shadowed or allegorized in the heathen mythology, as the first Cupid springing from the Egg of Night, the marriage of Cupid and Psyche, the Rape of Proserpine, the Congress of Jupiter and Juno, Death and Resuscitation of Adonis. . . . The Egyptians were possessed of many discoveries in philosophy and chemistry before the invention of letters; these were then expressed in hieroglyphic paintings of men and animals; which after the discovery of the alphabet were described and animated by the poets, and became first the deities of Egypt, and afterwards of Greece and Rome. Allusions to those fables were therefore thought proper ornaments to a philosophical poem, and are occasionally introduced either as represented by the poets, or preserved on the numerous gems and medallions of antiquity.[17]

Although Darwin calls these stories "ornaments" and says that they are only "occasionally introduced," this disclaimer is deceptive and probably even a conscious, comic concealment of the serious purpose of this poem and the others. First, the frequency with which serious and scholarly explanations of the truth expressed by these stories creep into his notes suggests that they were more than mere ornaments to Darwin. Second, his understanding of the mysteries themselves would require him to be secretive and evasive if he were presenting a modern, versed equivalent to them. We know that he understood this necessity in his note on the Portland vase since mysteries were traditionally presented evasively, and this evasive secrecy is implied in his veiled statement of purpose in a note early in *The Temple of Nature*: "Might not such a dignified pantomime be contrived, even at this age, as might strike the spectators with awe, and at the same time explain many philosophical truths by adapted imagery, and thus both amuse and instruct?"[18]

Although Primer reads only *The Temple of Nature* as a poem of serious themes veiled in secrecy, there is enough evidence to suggest that Darwin's knowledge of, and fascination with, the Eleusinian mysteries and his belief in myth extended further back into his writing career, and that all three of his poems can be read as integral parts of a "dignified pantomime" modeled on his understanding of the Eleusinian mysteries. Miss Seward tells us that he wrote "The Economy of Vegetation" first, and we will see that he included in it the same "hieroglyphic" stories and themes as appear in *The Temple of Nature*. But, as he realized more fully that he was writing modern-day mysteries (perhaps when he was doing the work for the verse and note on the Portland vase), he realized, I think, that he had to disguise them since all such "mystery" knowledge was traditionally only for the few: and this attempt explains in part the comic, ambiguous tone in all the poems. (The rest of the explanation lies with his overall philosophic position as described in Chapter 1.)

But, more specifically, this attempt explains the conception and publication of "The Loves of the Plants." When Darwin realized that he had to disguise the secrets of his philosophic poems, his "greater mysteries," he wrote a frivolous, nonsecret entertainment; and he published it first as "The Loves of the Plants," his "lesser mystery" which was intended to prepare the public for his more serious poems. In the note on the Portland vase, Darwin writes that "The exhibitions of the mysteries were of two kinds, those which the people were permitted to see, and those which were only shown to the initiated."[19] Then, in commenting to his friends about why he had published the second part of *The Botanic Garden* first, Darwin stated that "The Economy of Vegetation" was more difficult and that he needed to prepare his public. Anna Seward's description of this episode suggests his general deviousness and comic complexity:

> The Doctor was accustomed to remark, that whenever a strange step had been taken, if any way obnoxious to censure, the alleged reason was scarcely ever the real motive. His own singular management in this instance, and the way in which he accounted for it, proved a case in point. He was conscious that the second part of his work would be more level than the first to the comprehension, more congenial to the taste of the superficial reader, from it's [sic] being much less abstract and metaphysic, while it possessed more than sufficient poetic matter to entertain and charm the enlightened and judicious few. They, however, he well knew, when his first part should appear, would feel it's [sic] superiority to the earlier publication, it's [sic] grander conceptions, it's [sic] more splendid imagery, though less calculated to amuse and to be understood by common readers. Those of that last number who had purchased the first part would not like to possess the poem incomplete, and therefore would purchase the second. [20]

As I will show, the preparatory poem does include the same themes as the other two poems but in a more superficial and less developed state, just as the lesser Eleusinian mysteries were thought to anticipate the greater. Actually, the most frivolous and superficial segment of all three poems is the first canto of "The Loves of the Plants," which may mean only that it should be read as the lesser mystery and that the other three cantos of the poem are a kind of intermediate step between the lesser mystery and the genuinely greater mysteries of the philosophic poems.

In any case, Darwin's key poems are the two intended for the initiated: "The Economy of Vegetation" and *The Temple of Nature*. And the key ideas in these poems are hidden behind and within randomly placed stories with a comic tone. The great ideas, or themes, are circularity or the regeneration of new life from old;[21] marriage of different elements to each other and sexual love, which is both catalyst and binding force; and metamorphosis, which expresses not only the state of mortality but also the possibility of immortality through change into new forms. These themes are repeatedly allegorized in the stories he tells, and they are also given a certain scientific validity. His regeneration stories include the myths of Venus and Adonis, Orpheus and Eurydice, and the Phoenix. His marriage stories are often used as allegories for chemical reactions. The bonding power of love takes on cosmic and physical significance. And his stories of metamorphosis are both mythic and biological.

These themes are also symbolized in the structure of the poems and in the texture of the verse, not as systematically nor artfully as we might wish, but nevertheless symbolized. Rhetorical repetition and, in particular, the word patterning of chiasmus embody the theme of circularity, while the loose, disjointed plot structure of the poems embodies something like both circularity and metamorphosis, as I suggested in the previous chapter. Elizabeth Sewell's description of the structure of Ovid's *Metamorphoses* can apply to Darwin's poems as well, in kind if not in quality: "The profusion of connection and disconnection is not due to accident or failure of skill; it is a marvelous correspondence with the poet's subject matter. This is exactly what, from one point of view, the world is— a seemingly endless series of stories. . . ."[22]

Finally, like the eternal secrets of any mystery religion, which would neither be understood nor accepted by ordinary, complacent, small-minded men, these truths are concealed under a ludicrous, half-serious tone. In a sense, Darwin himself as a selfish man-in-society cannot face these secrets squarely; he directs the mockery at himself. In this self-mockery and concealment he reminds us of Lord Byron: he believes, but he cannot believe completely seriously. Thus, like so many post-Renaissance writers from Cervantes to John Barth, Darwin is genuinely comic; he protects what little belief he has by concealing it.

III   *The Lesser Mystery of "The Loves of the Plants" (1789)*

The most sensible scheme for dealing with the poems from this point on, I think, is to analyze large segments from each; but the chapter on his prose will be sandwiched between the two earlier poems and the last poem for reasons of chronology and pacing. This analysis will illustrate that the random stories do express a few simple theses and that thus there is a hidden structure or progression throughout Darwin's major poems that is modeled on the analogy of a mystery religion presentation and that presents definite thematic statements. Naturally, I choose the passages that are the best "hieroglyphs" for the themes and leave parts of the poems unmentioned. Some of these less successful passages could be said to be part of the evasive strategy of the poem, but I cannot argue this honestly for all of them. Darwin seems to have padded many of his cantos and to have failed on the side of verbosity—not in individual stories where his lavish diction and visual imagery serve a purpose—because he did not prune his lush vegetation of examples adequately. We do not deny, however, that in some of the stories there is a thematic pattern and a significant relation between form and content that this discussion unveils.

If a modern edition of Darwin's complete major poems is ever published, "The Loves of the Plants" should be placed first.[23]   In the opening canto, the stories are shorter and the tone is lighter than in any of the other poems, as we have already noted. Yet the themes set in "The Loves of the Plants" continually recur in the other poems. The theme of marriage and the personification of natural processes as love relationships, involving both fidelity and flirtatious infidelity as in human affairs, is implied by the title and appears continuously in the catalogue of the plants. The theme of circularity or regeneration is also anticipated by Darwin in this light, frivolous poem by the alternation both within cantos and between cantos of stories dealing with life and of ones dealing with death. This variation is done rather haphazardly, but nevertheless there is the impression of cyclical recurrence and regeneration in nature.

The relationship of these themes of love and circularity to each other is also apparent in Darwin's handling of his ostensible subject here, the erotic life of plants. Not only the obvious relationship that regeneration occurs through sexual union, but also the playful, facetious idea that "kissing" and "touching" constitute circular connections between otherwise unconnected things can be seen in his little cameos of flirtatious love.[24] The third theme, metamorphosis, is treated explicitly in the final canto of the poem and implicitly throughout. The personification of the plants is in itself a metamorphosis; any death and any rebirth are changes of form; and all of the love relationships have the power to change the partners as well as to create new forms.

At the beginning of the poem, Darwin tells us that metamorphosis is his most all-embracing theme, but he does so in a facetious tone: "Whereas P. Ovidius Naso, a great Necromancer in the famous Court of Augustus Caesar, did by art poetic transmute Men, Women, and even Gods and Goddesses, into Trees and Flowers; I have undertaken by similar art to restore some of them to their original animality, after having remained prisoners so long in their respective vegetable mansions."[25]

Even though "The Loves of the Plants" does embody each of these themes—in an embryonic state with a playful tone, and thus may be interpreted as a preparatory lesser mystery—the poem is lacking in memorable passages and is the least successful of the three. At the end of Canto I, there is a description of the metamorphosis in death of the Tremella, which Anna Seward claimed "is superior to the [description of the] Ovidian Daphne."[26] But compared to later stories, it is not worth detailed analysis. In Canto II, Darwin's treatment of the Egyptian Papyra plant expresses the hieroglyphic or symbolic powers of the written word; but neither the verse nor the notes tell the reader as much about Darwin's serious purpose as the later passages on the mystery religions do. I suggest that he could have packed this passage as full of references and meaning as the comparable passages in the later poems, since he wrote this poem after "The Economy of Vegetation," but that he deliberately withheld information here and made the references sketchy in order to keep the poem light. On the other hand, the relationship of thickly textured artifice to verbal symbolism is implied in this passage by the high concentration of chiasmus.[27] Thus, the reader is led part way into the mysteries, but he is not bombarded with meaning as he is in the later two poems.

At the end of Canto IV, that is, just before the conclusion of this preparatory lesser mystery, the theme of metamorphosis is presented several times in memorable, fully developed ways in the verse although wide-ranging, philosophic notes are withheld throughout the poem. And the last episode of the poem expresses both the regeneration theme and the marriage theme as they are made possible by metamorphosis. This episode includes references to both Proteus and Adonis, although the allegory is not elaborated as it later is; it tells a long story of flirtation and ends in a marriage; but it also suggests that the marriage is not an end point and that the loves are circular, continually renewing themselves in infidelity:

> *   *Where cool'd by rills, and curtain'd round by woods,*
> * *Slopes the green dell to meet the briny floods,*
> *The sparkling noon-beams trembling on the tide,*
> *The Proteus-Lover woos his playful bride,*
> *To win the fair he tries a thousand forms,*
> * *Basks on the sands, or gambols in the storms.*

> *A Dolphin now, his scaly sides he laves,*
> *And bears sportive Damsel on the waves;*
> *She strikes the cymbal as he moves along,*
> *And wondering Ocean listens to the song.*
> *—And now a spotted Pard the lover stalks,*
> * *Plays round her steps, and guards her favour'd walks;*
> *As with white teeth he prints her hand, caress'd,*
> *And lays his velvet paw upon her breast,*
> *O'er his round face her snowy fingers strain*
> *The silken knots, and fit the ribbon-rein.*
> *—And now a Swan, he spreads his plumy sails,*
> *And proudly glides before the fanning gales;*
> *Pleas'd on the flowery brink with graceful hand*
> *She waves her floating lover to the land;*
> *Bright shines his sinous neck, with crimson beak*
> *He prints fond kisses on her glowing cheek,*
> * *Spreads his broad wings, elates his ebon crest,*
> *And clasps the beauty to his downy breast.*
> *   A hundred *virgins join a* hundred *swains,*
> *And fond* ADONIS *leads the sprightly trains;*
> *Pair after pair, along his sacred groves*
> *To Hymen's fane the bright procession moves;*
> *Each smiling youth a myrtle garland shades,*
> *And wreaths of roses veil the blushing maids;*
> *Light Joys on twinkling feet attend the throng,*
> * *Weave the gay dance, or raise the frolic song;*
> *—Thick, as they pass, exulting Cupids fling*
> *Promiscuous arrows from the sounding string;*
> *On wings of gossamer soft Whispers fly,*
> *And the sly glance steals side-long from the eye.*
> *—As round his shrine the gawdy circles bow,*
> *And steal with muttering lips the faithless vow,*
> *Licentious Hymen joins their mingled hands,*
> *And loosely twines the meretricious bands.—*
> *Thus where pleased* VENUS, *in the southern main,*
> *Sheds all her smiles on Otaheite's plain,*
> *Wide o'er the isle her silken net she draws,*
> *And the Loves laugh at all but Nature's laws.*[28]

The "secret" embodied in this little story has to do with the continual flexibility and vitality of life, one which has a kind of erotic energy. In the texture of the verse here, the circularity is symbolized by straight parallelism rather than chiasmus, since there is no interplay between the two devices; and I have marked each line that contains this parallelism with an asterisk. The poetic diction and visual imagery of a phrase like "the flowery brink" (1.483) expresses the gaudiness of nature. And the sheer silliness of a phrase like "Light Joys on twinkling feet" (1. 495) keeps the tone facetious enough so that the reader can choose not to notice the serious statement of the passage: nature's vitality transcends the conservative mores of men. This concept is a bit terrifying, as a note reminds us that some primitive societies are more "natural" than ours: "The society, called the Areoi, in the island of Otaheite, consists of about 100 males and 100 females, who form one promiscuous marriage."[29] Thus, Darwin has presented a "scenical representation" for part of his "secret" while at the same time concealing his meaning behind playfulness.

IV *The Greater Mystery of "The Economy of Vegetation" (1791–92)*

Although the explicit use of the Eleusinian mysteries as an organization principle does not appear until Darwin's final poem, "The Economy of Vegetation," this companion poem to "The Loves of the Plants" contains a breadth of purpose and an abundance of ambitious "scenical representations" that classify it with *The Temple of Nature*. The Botanic Goddess in "The Economy of Vegetation" resembles the Hierophant of the mysteries in the later poem. For the initiated—those of us who struggle with the verse and the notes—the Goddess's explanations lead to scientific truths as well as a deeper understanding of the recurring philosophic themes. Darwin has her speak to personified representatives of one of the four elements of fire, earth, water, and air in each of four cantos. (Canto I was minutely paraphrased earlier in this chapter.) But at any one point all of the basic themes can appear since the intermingling and the uniformity of physical phenomena are the same anywhere we find them.[30]

In a letter in which he says that this poem "is so deep, that I cannot read six lines together and know what they are about, till I have studied them in the long notes," Horace Walpole commends highly Darwin's picture of the creation of the universe.[31] The passage is in Canto I, but I also quote the six lines prior to those which Walpole admired:

"NYMPHS OF PRIMEVAL FIRE! YOUR *vestal train*
*   Hung with gold-tresses o'er the vast inane,*
      Pierced with your silver shafts the throne of Night,
      And charm'd young Nature's opening eyes with light;
      When LOVE DIVINE, *with brooding wings unfurl'd,*
      Call'd from the rude abyss the living world.
      "—LET THERE BE LIGHT!" *proclaim'd the* ALMIGHTY LORD,
      Astonish'd Chaos heard the potent word;—
      Through all his realms the kindling Ether runs,
*   And the mass starts into a million suns;*
      Earths round each sun with quick explosions burst,
*   And second planets issue from the first;*
*   Bend, as they journey with projectile force,*
*   In bright ellipses their reluctant course;*
      Orbs wheel in orbs, round centres centres roll,
      And form, self-balanced, one revolving Whole.
      —Onward they move amid their bright abode,
*   Space without bound,* THE BOSOM OF THEIR GOD !³²

Although we can never know how complete an initiate Walpole
became, he could have discovered in the rest of the poem the
reworking of the basic themes which are figured here. Vivid circularity, explosive metamorphosis, and a personified love force that
is flirtatious and sexy as well as motherly constitute Darwin's
visual presentation of the "big bang" theory of the universe. The
meter, verging on strong-stress patterns in some lines, suggests
balance and circularity: there are six four-stress lines, the ones
marked with asterisks. The image in the last line especially expresses
the recurrent themes: the universe is a "bosom." Thus it is "curved"
(later in *The Temple of Nature* Darwin associates the beauty of
curved lines with the female bosom and bases his theory on
Hogarth's notion); it is sexy; and, at the same time, it is motherly.
The fact that God seems to become a mother with a female bosom is
part of an hermaphroditism that runs through the poems. The muse
in the last poem may be both male and female. This hermaphroditism
produces a facetious tone which is part of the comic evasiveness,
but it is also consistent with the theme of metamorphosis. Sex,
like all form in nature, is not fixed but flexible.³³

Finally, in one of several notes appended to this passage, Darwin
suggests part of the scientific truth that his images allegorize: "*When
Love Divine. 1. 101.* From having observed the gradual evolution

of the young animal or plant from its egg or seed; and afterwards its successive advances to its more perfect state, or maturity; philosophers of all ages seem to have imagined, that the great world itself had likewise its infancy and its gradual progress to maturity; this seems to have given origin to the very antient and sublime allegory of Eros, or Divine Love, producing the world from the egg of Night, as it floated in Chaos."[34]

A key idea in his use of allegorical stories is the notion that this "Divine Love" continues to function after creation in the interaction of physical phenomena. Science calls these interactions geological formations, chemical reactions, plant reproductions, and so on. The conception of "The Loves of the Plants" prefigures this idea, but Darwin illustrates it in more elaborated allegorical stories here. Canto II includes a description of the geological formation of continents which is allegorized as Venus rising from the sea, and she is beautiful and seductive. The last eight lines of the thirty-four-line passage are followed by the explanatory note:

> The bright drops, rolling from her lifted arms,
> In slow meanders wander o'er her charms
> Seek round her snowy neck their lucid track,
> Pearl her white shoulders, gem her ivory back,
> Round her fine waist and swelling bosom swim,
> And star with glittering brine each crystal limb.—
> —The immortal form enamour'd Nature hail'd,
> And Beauty blazed to heaven and earth, unvail'd.

So young Dione. 1. 47. There is an antient gem representing Venus rising out of the ocean supported by two Tritons. From the formality of the design it would appear to be of great antiquity before the introduction of fine taste into the world. It is probable that this beautiful allegory was originally an hieroglyphic picture (before the invention of letters) descriptive of the formation of the earth from the ocean, which seems to have been an opinion of many of the most antient philosophers.[33]

Later in the canto an illicit love affair is used as an allegory for the chemical reaction of nitric acid with oxygen to produce what is probably a nitrate salt. During the course of this reaction, a reddish vapor is given off and heat escapes; and Darwin likens this result to Mars's seduction of Venus and to Vulcan's ensuing anger, which ties them together with a net, that is, the chemical bond. The point of the story, which is a nicely told little anecdote, is not to make a specific statement about any one chemical reaction but rather to show that chemical bonds are tight, netlike affairs, which also change rapidly: they go from one "lover" to another. The passage also contains more than the average amount of chiasmus (five lines in a passage of thirty-two lines, marked here with asterisks), which suggests circularity, or, in this case, fickleness:

> So Beauty's Goddess, warm with new desire
> Left, on her silver wheels, the God of Fire;
> Her faithless charms to fiercer Mars resign'd,
> * Met with fond lips, with wanton arms intwin'd.
> —Indignant Vulcan eyed the parting Fair,
> And watch'd with jealous step the guilty pair;
> O'er his broad neck a wiry net he flung,
> Quick as he strode, tinkling meshes rung;
> Fine as the spider's flimsy thread He wove
> The immortal toil to lime illicit love;
> Steel were the knots, and steel the twisted thong,
> Ring link'd in ring, indissolubly strong;
> On viewless hooks along the fretted roof
> He hung, unseen, the inextricable woof.—
> * —Quick start the springs, the webs pellucid spread,
> And lock the embracing Lovers on their bed;
> Fierce with loud taunts vindictive Vulcan springs,
> Tries all the bolts, and tightens all the strings,
> Shakes with incessant shouts the bright abodes,
> Claps his rude hands, and calls the festive Gods.—
> —With spreading palms the alarmed Goddess tries
> To veil her beauties from celestial eyes,
> * Writhes her fair limbs, the slender ringlets strains,
> And bids her loves untie the obdurate chains;
> Soft swells her panting bosom, as she turns,
> And her flush'd cheek with brighter blushes burns.
> Majestic grief the Queen of Heaven avows,
> And chaste Minerva hides her helmed brows;
> * Attendant Nymphs with bashful eyes askance
> Steal of intangled Mars a transient glance;
> Surrounding Gods the circling nectar quaff,
> * Gaze on the Fair, and envy as they laugh.[36]

A combination of geological phenomena and chemical phenomena is allegorized by Darwin a little farther on in this canto with another sexy love story from mythology. Jove's rapes of mortal women, especially Europa, serve as an allegory for the production of various fine earths through the chemical decomposition and then oxidation of material such as sulphur. Jove is oxygen, and in Darwin's story he has affairs with Hebe, Leda, Olympia, and finally Europa. This episode, which extends for fifty-five lines, embodies all three themes of love, metamorphosis, and regeneration. Darwin's note illustrates the interaction of myth and science in his thought:

Inconstant Jove. 1. 299. The purer air or ether in the antient mythology was represented by Jupiter, and the inferior air by Juno; and the conjunction of these deities was said to produce the vernal showers, and procreate all things, as is further spoken of in Canto III, 1. 204. It is now discovered that pure air, or oxygene, uniting with variety of bases forms the various kinds of acids; as the vitriolic acid from pure air and sulphur; the nitrous acid from pure air and phlogistic air, or azote [nitrogen]; and carbonic acid, (or fixed air,) from pure air and charcoal. Some of these affinities were perhaps portrayed by the Magi of Egypt, who were probably learned in chemistry, in their hieroglyphic pictures before the invention of letters, by the loves of Jupiter with terrestrial ladies. And thus physically as well as metaphysically might be said "*Jovis omnia plena.*"[37]

One of the most successful seduction stories of this kind is the one in Canto III that the above note directs us to: the story of Juno's enticement or recapture of the affections of her flirtatious husband, Jupiter, allegorizes the chemical reaction of oxygen and hydrogen to form water. Scientific opinion of Darwin's day apparently held the misconception that such a reaction was partially responsible for rain; therefore, the following story is a figure not only for chemical phenomena but also for meteorological. As is typical of his organization in most of these stories, Darwin first gives a personified description of the physical event and then moves into an extended allegorical simile:

> "NYMPHS! YOUR *bright squadrons watch with chemic eyes*
> *The cold-elastic vapours, as they rise;*
> *With playful force arrest them as they pass,*
> *And to pure* AIR *betroth the flaming* GAS.
> *Round their translucent forms at once they fling*
> *Their rapturous arms, with silver bosoms cling;*
> *In fleecy clouds their flutterings wings extend,*
> *Or from the skies in lucid showers descend;*
> *Whence rills and rivers owe their secret birth.*
> *And Ocean's hundred arms unfold the earth.*
>
> "*So, robed by Beauty's Queen, with softer charms*
> SATURNIA *woo'd the Thunderer to her arms;*
> *O'er her fair limbs a veil of light she spread,*

And bound a starry diadem on her head;
Long braids of pearl her golden tresses grac'd,
And the charm'd CESTUS sparkled round her waist.
* —Raised o'er the woof, by Beauty's hand inwrought,
Breathes the soft Sigh, and glows the enamour'd Thought;
Vows on light wings succeed, and quiver'd Wiles,
Assuasive Accents, and seductive Smiles.
—Slow rolls the Cyprian car in purple pride,
And, steer'd by LOVE, ascends admiring Ide;
* Climbs the green slopes, the nodding woods pervades,
Burns round the rocks, or gleams amid the shades.—
Glad ZEPHR leads the train, and waves above
The barbed darts, and blazing torch of Love;
* Reverts his smiling face, and pausing flings
Soft showers of roses from aurelian wings.
* Delighted Fawns, in wreathes of flowers array'd,
With tiptoe Wood-Boys beat the chequer'd glade;
Alarmed Naiads, rising into air,
Lift o'er their silver urns their leafy hair;
Each to her oak the bashful Dryads shrink,
And azure eyes are seen through every chink.
—LOVE culls a flaming shaft of broadest wing,
And rests the fork upon the quivering string;
Points his arch eye aloft, with fingers strong
Draws to his curled ear the silken thong;
* Loud twangs the steel, the golden arrow flies,
Trails a long line of lustre through the skies;
"'Tis done!" he shouts, "the mighty Monarch feels!"
And with loud laughter shakes the silver wheels;
Bends o'er the car, and whirling, as it moves,
His loosen'd bowstring, drives the rising doves.
—Pierced on his throne the starting Thunderer turns,
* Melts with soft sighs, with kindling rapture burns;
Clasps her fair hand, and eyes in fond amaze
The bright Intruder with enamour'd gaze.
"And leaves my Goddess, like a blooming bride,
"The fanes of Argos for the rocks of Ide?
"Her gorgeous palaces, and amaranth bowers,
"For cliff-top'd mountains, and aerial towers?"
He said; and, leading from her ivory seat
The blushing Beauty to his lone retreat,
Curtain'd with night the couch imperial shrouds,
And rests the crimson cushions upon clouds.—
Earth feels the grateful influence from above,

> * *Sighs the soft Air, and Ocean murmurs love;*
> *Etherial Warmth expands his brooding wing,*
> *And in still showers descends the genial Spring.*

And in still showers. 1. 260. The allegorical interpretation of the very antient mythology which supposes Jupiter to represent the superior part of the atmosphere or ether, and Juno the inferior air, and that the conjunction of these two produced vernal showers, as alluded to in Virgil's Georgics, is so analogous to the present important discovery of the production of water from pure air, or oxygene, and inflammable air, or hydrogen, (which from its greater levity probably resides over the former,) that one should be tempted to believe that the very antient chemists of Egypt had discovered the composition of water, and thus represented it in their hieroglyphic figures before the invention of letters.[38]

I have marked with asterisks in the above passage the lines which contain reverse parallelism, or chiasmus, which is more frequent here than in any other segment of Darwin's verse, although it is almost as frequent in the Venus and Mars story quoted above. Combined with straight parallelism and the images themselves, chiasmus expresses the theme of cyclical patterns or circularity which is so important in a description of the water cycle. Not only is there vertical circularity in the fact of water going up and coming down, but there is also horizontal circularity suggested when the Botanic Goddess notices that the oceans "infold the earth" (1.210). In fact, the whole passage seems to resemble Percy B. Shelley's description of the water cycle in "The Cloud" with one major difference: Shelley's poem is more subtle in its nearly metaphysical imagery while, Darwin's broad allegory has a more interesting effect of tone. The chemical and meteorological reaction allegorized by Juno and Jupiter is erotic and thus strong, which is a good simile for the turbulence of the sky; but it is also rather funny in the sly way that Darwin hints that the rain may be associated with the resulting sexual orgasm. Darwin's understanding of the cycles and forces in nature is profound, but it is also at the same time detached. He is the mysterious Hierophant, revealing and concealing in the same figure; he is the comic poet and philosopher, like Byron, who believes but fears to do so.

In Canto IV, Darwin, when he returns to the chemical reaction of oxygen and hydrogen, again uses the metaphor of marriage. This time the myth is different, the marriage of Cupid and Psyche; and the reaction is not so elaborately or so interestingly presented as in the previous passage. But the accompanying personified descriptions of the reaction are clear statements of the three themes of love, circularity, and metamorphosis. The lines, with the story left out, indicate the themes:

> *You [the sylphs of air] form with chemic hands the airy surge,*
> *Mix with broad vans, with shadowy tridents urge.*
> SYLPHS! *from each sun-bright leaf, that twinkling shakes*
> *O'er Earth's green lap, or shoots amid her lakes,*
> *Your playful bands with simpering lips invite,*
> *And wed the enamour'd* OXYGENE *to* LIGHT. —
> *Round their white necks with fingers interwove,*
> *Cling the fond Pair with unabating love;*
> *Hand link'd in hand on buoyant step they rise,*
> *And soar and glisten in unclouded skies.*
> *Whence in bright floods the* VITAL AIR *expands,*
> *And with concentric spheres involves the lands;*
> *Pervades the swarming seas, and heaving earths,*
> *Where teeming Nature broods her myriad births;*
> *Fills the fine lungs of all that* breathe *or* bud,
> *Warms the new heart, and dyes the gushing blood;*
> *With Life's first spark inspires the organic frame,*
> *And, as it wastes, renews the subtle flame.*
>
> *"So pure, so soft, with sweet attraction shone*
> *Fair Psyche, . . ."*
> —*Hence plastic Nature, as Oblivion whelms*
> *Her fading forms, repeoples all her realms;*
> *Soft Joys disport on purple plumes unfurl'd.*
> *And love and Beauty rule the willing world.*[39]

The phrase "plastic Nature" and the lines following it constitute a fine expression of both metamorphosis and regeneration, while the images in the earlier lines stress circularity and love.

If there are three recurring themes in Darwin's poems, they are all related to one prime interest: birth. This relationship, or emphasis, is not surprising since Darwin was a doctor. It has also been said of a modern poet who was a doctor by profession, William Carlos Williams, that the subject which preoccupied him most was birth.[40] Each of the three themes, which I have been following in Darwin's poems, is embodied in the fact of birth; and there is an alliterative phrase that he likes well enough to repeat several times that refers all at once to sexual birth, regeneration, and meta-

morphosis: "buds or breathes." It appears slightly modified above;
it appears in *The Temple of Nature*; it also appears at the end of one
of the most effective passages of "The Economy of Vegetation"
near the end of Canto IV:

> "SYLPHS! *as you hover on ethereal wing,*
> *Brood the green children of parturient Spring!—*
> *Where in their bursting cells my Embryons rest,*
> *I charge you guard the vegetable nest;*
> *Count with nice eye the myriad* SEEDS, *that swell*
> *Each vaulted womb of husk, or pod, or shell;*
> *Feed with sweet juices, clothe with downy hair,*
> *Or hang, inshrined, their little orbs in air.*
>   "*So, late decry'd by* HERSCHEL'S *piercing sight,*
> *Hand the bright squadrons of the twinkling Night;*
> *Ten thousand marshall'd stars, a silver zone,*
> *Effuse their blended lustres round her throne;*
> *Suns call to suns, in lucid clouds conspire,*
> *And light exterior skies with golden fire;*
> *Resistless rolls the illimitable sphere,*
> *And one great circle forms the unmeasured year.*
> —*Roll on,* YE STARS! *exult in youthful prime,*
> *Mark with bright curves the printless steps of Time;*
> *Near and more near your beamy cars approach,*
> *And lessening orbs on lessening orbs encroach;—*
> *Flowers of the sky! ye too to age must yield,*
> *Frail as your silken sisters of the field!*
> *Star after star from Heaven's high arch shall rush,*
> *Suns sink on suns, and systems systems crush,*
> *Headlong, extinct, to one dark centre fall,*
> *And Death and Night and Chaos mingle all!*
> —*Till o'er the wreck, emerging from the storm,*
> *Immortal* NATURE *lifts her changeful form,*
> *Mounts from her funeral pyre on wings of flame,*
> *And soars and shines, another and the same.*
>
>   2. "*Lo! on each* SEED *within its slender rind*
> *Life's golden threads in endless circles wind;*
> *Maze within maze the lucid webs are roll'd,*
> *And, as they burst, the living flame unfold.*
> *The pulpy acorn, ere it swells, contains*
> *The Oak's vast branches in its milky veins;*
> *Each ravel'd bud, fine film, and fibre-line*
> *Traced with nice pencil on the small design.*
> *The young Narcissus, in it's bulb compress'd,*

Cradles a second nestling on its breast;
In whose fine arms a younger embryon lies,
Folds its thin leaves, and shuts its floret-eyes;
Grain within grain successive harvests dwell,
And boundless forests slumber in a shell.
—So yon grey precipice, and ivy'd towers,
Long winding meads, and intermingled bowers,
Green files of poplars, o'er the lake that bow,
And glimmering wheel, which rolls and foams below,
In one bright point with nice distinction lie
Plan'd on the moving tablet of the eye.
—So, fold on fold, Earth's wavy plains extend,
And, sphere in sphere, its hidden strata bend;—
Incumbent Spring her beamy plumes expands
O'er restless oceans, and impatient lands,
With genial lustres warms the mighty ball,
And the GREAT SEED *evolves, disclosing* ALL*;*
LIFE *buds or breathes from Indus to the Poles,*
And the vast surface kindles, as it rolls![41]

This passage is a lyric celebration of birth: astronomical birth, plant birth, animal birth, and geological birth. The predominant myth in the passage is that of the first great egg of night from which "Divine Love" produced the universe. Darwin had alluded to this myth early in Canto I, and he now puts together a beautifully intricate development of the idea at the end of the poem.[42] The image of the egg itself suggests circularity, and Darwin emphasizes this shape by noticing circularity first in tiny seeds, then in astronomical solar systems, then in seeds again, then in the human eye, and finally in terrestrial geography. Everything is round and spinning: a figure both for continual regeneration and metamorphosis. Also, the function of the egg, as well as all the referents just mentioned, represents continual metamorphosis. The theme of love and marriage is not worked out explicitly in the passage, but in a sense the entire thing is a celebration of the power of love. The passage moves wonderfully from the microcosm to the macrocosm, and it blends the image of tiny circular seeds to the image of swirling stars around the rubrics of circularity and metamorphosis. It is intricate and evasive because of its thick verbal texture, and yet at the same time Darwin treats this subject very seriously indeed. Along with a few other passages, including the seduction scenes quoted earlier in this section, this celebration of birth is Darwin at his poetic best.

CHAPTER 3

Science Writing on a Grand Scale

THE writer who wanted to celebrate the fecundity of life as well as the natural philosopher who simply wanted to describe life systems often used an elegant and energetic prose as his medium—at least until slightly less than a century ago when the symbolic language of mathematics became the medium for science.[1] Erasmus Darwin contributed two large and fascinating books to this literature of scientific prose, *Zoonomia* (1794–96) and *Phytologia* (1800). Like the more familiar books of his grandson that produced a kind of climax to this genre of scientific prose, Darwin's treatises can, and should, be appreciated as imaginative literature. Such an appreciation cannot comprehend and explain their contributions to science, but it does describe them as organizations of imaginative themes and tones consistent with Darwin's other writings.

In a brilliant piece of literary criticism of Charles Darwin's scientific prose, Stanley Edgar Hyman makes these same qualifications on his method by saying that he is just a student of literature, but he then justifies the literary study of a book like Charles Darwin's *The Origin of the Species*: "Any book of ideas is to some degree metaphoric; a great book of ideas consists of profound metaphors in a realized form, analogous to the traditional forms of literature. If these metaphors are sometimes shocking and surrealistic—the children spun into silk, the cauldron of seething excitement—they are sometimes the ultimate commonplaces we have always known—the tangled bank of life, the web of thought."[2] Erasmus Darwin's scientific prose is not so great, either as science or as prose, as that of his grandson; but that his prose does leave a significant imaginative impression should not be ignored.

The tradition for this kind of writing, which extended from the seventeenth-century founders of the Royal Society through Charles Darwin, required that the prose exhibit straightforward simplicity as well as a comprehensiveness and generality that would express unifying concepts for all nature. The editors of an anthology of this scientific prose describe well these two characteristics of it: "The aim of the reform [in prose style during the seventeenth century] was plainness and simplicity. Simplicity, however, is not enough to explain the excellence of the scientific writers, selections from whom are given in this collection. The quality of largeness characteristic of English prose about science until relatively recent decades is obviously something more than a product of simplicity."[3] In other words, the tradition of science writing in prose, to which Darwin belongs, included a kind of religious comprehensiveness, or "largeness," as a prime characteristic. Stanley Edgar Hyman finds this characteristic manifested in the younger Darwin: "The appeal of the *Origin* is not only for imagination, wonder, marvel, rather than ratiocination, but ultimately for belief and faith."[4]

Many of the science writers were, of course, Deists; but Erasmus Darwin, I believe, was not, as I have explained in Chapter 1. Thus, the metaphors and imaginative constructs to be found in his prose are more consistently "large" because he does not fall back on the simplifying "watch-maker" generalization of the Deists; instead, he tries to find unifying concepts for an infinitely complex materialism. And, even though he fails scientifically, the overall literary effect is one of energy, belief, and awe in the face of a marvelously fecund nature that is not by any means exclusively human or anthropomorphic. Furthermore, these volumes of serious description of nature help to explain the comic tone of detachment elsewhere in Darwin's writing. The "web of thought" about nature that we can unravel from his prose treatises does not allow much anthropomorphism, and yet Darwin loves "man"—hence the comic devices and comic tone that we find in the poems.

I   Zoonomia *(1794–96)*

The subtitle of the first volume of *Zoonomia* is *The Laws of Organic Life*, while the second volume, published two years after the first, is a catalogue of all human diseases. *Zoonomia* volumes 1 and 2 is a huge book, and the editions that I have seen have none of the "flowery" prettiness of the books of poems, since Darwin's *Zoonomia* is a long and serious exposition of his materialism. First, he describes the mechanism of all aspects of animal life from the movement of blood through the blood vessels to the movement of ideas in the brain. In order to make such a comprehensive description, he has to posit a force or a phenomenon in nature that he labels "animal motion." Based on this comprehensive description, then, of the mechanism of animal life, Darwin can classify and suggest cures for all known human diseases, the purpose of his second volume. Given such rigid systematizing, he classifies, of course, many activities as diseases which are not normally considered undesirable, such as reverie, ambition, and even sleep. In short, Darwin's treatise on animal, and particularly on human, life is absurdly wrong in many ways; but it is so because of its "largeness," its attempt to explain all things. This largeness, however, makes it enjoyably human reading as well as provocatively far-sighted in some areas, such as evolution.

The preface to *Zoonomia* is an acccurate foretaste of the scope of the book and a good example of the straightforward yet large prose. In the first paragraph, Darwin gives a hint of how important the notion of "animal motion" or animation will be, and the next paragraph explains how important reasoning by analogy is to one who wants to discover unities:

> The purport of the following pages is an endeavour to reduce the facts belonging to ANIMAL LIFE into classes, orders, genera, and species; and, by comparing them with each other, to unravel the theory of diseases. It happened, perhaps unfortunately for the inquirers into the knowledge of diseases, that other sciences had received improvement previous to their own; whence, instead of comparing the properties belonging to animated nature with each other, they, idly ingenious, busied themselves in attempting to explain the laws of life by those of mechanism and chemistry; they considered the body as an hydraulic machine, and the fluids as passing through a series of chemical changes, forgetting that animation was its essential characteristic.
>
> The great CREATOR of all things has infinitely diversified the works of his hands, but has at the same time stamped a certain similitude on the features of nature, that demonstrates to us, that *the whole is one family of one parent*. On this similitude is founded all rational analogy; which, so long as it is concerned in comparing the essential properties of bodies, leads us to many and important discoveries; but when with licentious activity it links together objects, otherwise discordant, by some fanciful similitude; it may indeed collect ornaments for wit and poetry, but philosophy and truth recoil from its combinations.[5]

The comic tension of believing and yet not believing that is so characteristic of Darwin's poetry seems to creep into the passage above. He is at odds with himself because he depends greatly on speculative analogy and yet would prefer more certainty. Actually, the most interesting sections in his prose are those in which he goes out on a speculative limb; for he does so with gusto while all the time preferring the true center of certainty.

Darwin's most daring attempt in *Zoonomia* to explain a mystery is his explanation of the linkage between sense impressions and the total life of the organism—a mystery that physiologists and psychologists are still trying to explain. Why is it that we pay attention to certain sense impressions, build them into ideas which determine our actions, while we ignore other sense impressions? In short, what exactly are ideas? In order to explain this mystery, Darwin has to invent another mystery, a "*je ne sais quoi*," and then analyze, subdivide, and label his invention. He calls his explanatory concept "animal motion," or the spirit of animation, which is a phenomenon possessed by all living matter; in fact, the possession of animal motion is what makes matter "living." He insists that this power is different from mechanical or chemical power; it is something else: "Hence, when we say animal motion is excited by irritation, we do not mean that the motion bears any proportion to the mechanical impulse of the stimulus; not that it is affected by the general gravitation of the two bodies; nor by their chemical properties, but solely that certain animal fibres are excited into action by something external to the moving organ."[6]

In other words, Darwin does not believe in passive organs that are merely acted upon by external stimuli; the organs themselves perform animal motion. He tries to prove the existence of this force in nature by detailed psychological observation, and some of his illustrations seem convincing—such as his description of the fact that, as one looks at something, the perception becomes weaker, thereby indicating something autonomous (not mechanical) about the organ of sight:

Now if the change or motion of the retina was a mechanical impression, or a chemical tinge of coloured light, the perception would every minute become stronger and stronger,—whereas in this experiment it becomes every instant weaker and weaker. . . .

Thus when a circular coin, as a shilling, is pressed on the palm of the hand, the sense of touch is mechanically compressed; but it is the stimulus of this pressure that excites the organ of touch into animal motion, which constitutes the perception of hardness and of figure: for in some minutes the perception ceases, though the mechanical pressure of the object remains.[7]

Working on the assumption that he has an all-purpose hypothesis, Darwin categorizes and speculates for pages. He divides animal motion into four different types: irritative, sensitive, voluntary, and associative, each with its own special definition and description.[8] He then explains how all "our ideas are animal motions of the organs of sense."[9]

This speculative writing is interesting as literature because Darwin seems now and then to be troubled by what might be regarded as the ontology of his explanations; and this produces, even in his scientific prose, the comic tension so characteristic of his writing. He is trying to give a mechanical, step-by-step "human" explanation of something that he knows is organic, too complex for human simplification, and thus unexplainable. He cannot just accept the fact of growth and organic development because that would be to submerge himself in dehumanizing natural flow, but, at the same time, he feels uneasy positing forces and explanations that sound distinctly metaphysical. He insists that animal motion is nothing more than a property of the material world, but he cannot just let it *be* in its organic complexity. In a sense, then, he personifies animal motion, just as he personifies elements and plants in his poems because, by personifying it, he can give its anatomy, its logically mechanical description. At the same time, however, he believes in the organic, description-defying reality of the phenomenon which makes his own efforts puny and absurd. When this comic tone of Darwin's is found in his highly speculative science writing, the writing comes alive, both as science and as human voice in the face of something far greater than science or humanity.

For example, his theory of animal motion sounds like a reiteration of the familiar distinction between spirit and matter, that is common in Western thought. In one passage, he even speculates that his theory may be a new argument for the existence of individual immortality. But, even though he toys with the notion of individual immortality (in a comic way?), he refuses to commit himself to the idea. Undoubtedly, life goes on, and animal motion does exist generally as a force in the universe; but such an existence is terrifyingly different from what individuals come to think of as their own individual immortality. Thus, Darwin's thinking does play with the notion of "spirit," but his honesty keeps it a strangely materialistic kind of spirit. The passage in question is a good example

of Darwin's continual comic stance of holding back a little bit from
the full implications of his thought:

> Nor is this theory [of immaterial forces] ill supported by analogy, since
> heat, electricity, and magnetism, can be given to or taken from a piece of
> iron; and must therefore exist, whether separated from the metal, or com-
> bined with it. From a parity of reasoning, the spirit of animation would ap-
> pear to be capable of existing as well as seperately from the body as with it.
>
> I beg to be understood, that I do not wish to dispute about words, and
> am ready to allow, that the powers of gravity, specific attraction, electricity,
> magnetism, and even the spirit of animation, may consist of matter of a
> finer kind. . . . [here he quotes from St. Paul] By the words spirit of anima-
> tion or sensorial power, I mean only that animal life, which mankind pos-
> sesses in common with brutes, and in some degree even with vegetables,
> and leave the consideration of the immortal part of us, which is the object
> of religion, to those who treat of revelation.[10]

At its best, his discussion of animal motion becomes a grand
metaphor for the infinitely complex and infinitely vital world of
fluxing matter, the world of continuous birth. In such a world,
man, even life itself, is just a momentary speck in the changing
scene. When his speculation carries him to such sublime images,
his prose loses the comic brittleness of human science and becomes
genuinely lyric. At his highest moments of vision, he does not care
that what he sees reduces man to nothing. His description of "self-
identity" is a good example of this lyric acceptance of absurdity,
against which he usually has a comic defense:

> Our identity is known by our acquired habits or catenated trains of
> ideas and muscular motions; and perhaps, when we compare infancy with
> old age, in those alone can our identity be supposed to exist. For what
> else is there of similitude between the first speck of living entity and the
> mature man—every deduction of reasoning, every sentiment or passion,
> with every fibre of the corporeal part of our system, has been subject almost
> to annual mutation; while some catenations alone of our ideas and muscular
> actions have continued in part unchanged . . . It is these habits of action,
> these catenations of ideas and muscular motions, which begin with life,
> and only terminate with it; and which we can in some measure deliver to
> our posterity; as explained in Sect. XXXIX. . . . So far are we governed by
> the catenations of motions, which affect both the body and the mind of
> man, and which begin with our irritability [a subdivision of animal motion],
> and end with it.[11]

The reference to Section, or Chapter, XXXIX, above is a reference to what is probably the most famous section in *Zoonomia*, "Of Generation." In elaborating his vision of continuing movement (catenation), he has to discard the traditional biological notion of fixed species; and he replaces it with a description of continual generation over vast expanses of time, the notion of progressive evolution. He oversimplifies in his description of the process of inheriting improved characteristics, but he does have a vision of the struggle for existence and of its relation to the generation and the survival of the fittest: "The final cause of this contest amongst the males seems to be, that the strongest and most active animal should propagate the species, which should thence become improved."[12] In addition to his mistake in thinking that improved traits are directly passed on, Darwin also had the false notion that all inherited traits come from the male and furthermore that, by force of will, the male could pass on certain traits to his offspring. In fact, near the end of this chapter about generation Darwin makes the wonderful suggestion that a school be formed to train men to procreate either males or females by the proper use of their imaginations.[13]

In spite of these errors, however, and without much experimental, supporting data, Darwin's speculations on the generation of life over time are thrillingly penetrating. There are long reaches of tedious writing, just as there are throughout the *Zoonomia*; but they are compensated for by passages of celebration such as the following:

From thus meditating on the great similarity of the structure of the warm-blooded animals, and at the same time of the great changes they undergo both before and after their nativity; and by considering in how minute a portion of time many of the changes of animals above described have been produced; would it be too bold to imagine, that in the great length of time, since the earth began to exist, perhaps millions of ages before the commencement of the history of mankind, would it be too bold to imagine, that all warmblooded animals have arisen from one living filament, which the Great First Cause endued with animality, with the power of acquiring new parts, attended with new propensities, directed by irritations, sensations, volitions, and associations [the subdivisions of animal motion]; and thus possessing the faculty of continuing to improve by its own inherent activity, and of delivering down those improvements by generation to its posterity, world without end! . . .

The late Mr. David Hume, in his posthumous works, places the powers of generation much above those of our boasted reason; and adds, that reason can only make a machine, as a clock or a ship, but the power of generation makes the maker of the machine; and probably from having observed, that the greatest part of the earth has been formed out of organic recrements; as the immense beds of limestone, chalk, sandstone, ironstone, coals, from decomposed vegetables; all which have been first produced by generation, or by the secretions of organic life; he concludes that the world itself might have been generated, rather than created; that is, it might have been gradually produced from very small beginnings, increasing by the activity of its inherent principles. . . .[14]

But it is not just the long sentences, the "largeness," and the celebration of generation that make Darwin's writing on the subject interesting; his descriptions hint strongly at the fact that there is a kind of human absurdity that appears when the implications of such thought are followed very far. For example, any theory of evolution must celebrate the death of individuals because there could be no improvement without death. Darwin's description of death is consistent with his theory of animal motion and is, in fact, a beautifully written description although somewhat macabre in its cool detachment:

On considering this subject [death] one should have imagined at first view, that it might have been easier for nature to have supported her progeny for ever in health and life, than to have perpetually reproduced them by the wonderful and mysterious process of generation. But it seems our bodies by long habit cease to obey the stimulus of the aliment, which should support us. After we have acquired our height and solidity we make no more new parts, and the system obeys the irritations, sensations, volitions, and associations, with less and less energy, till the whole sinks into inaction.[15]

Even more disturbing, however, to our beliefs in human worth, and in individuality is Darwin's blandly matter-of-fact speculation that there can be no such thing as a unique individual: "Owing to the imperfection of language the offspring is termed a *new* animal, but is in truth a branch or elongation of the parent; since a part of the embryon-animal is, or was, a part of the parent; and therefore in strict language it cannot be said to be entirely *new* at the time of its production; and therefore it may retain some of the habits of the parent-system."[16] Darwin's speculative writing invents models: it tries to describe coherent systems for all movement over time and space. Such descriptions, even though they may work beautifully as mechanical systems for describing and predicting phenomena (science), invariably are terrifying because, insofar as they work, they engulf the describer.

The dilemma of the speculative thinker, or scientist, who wants to give comprehensive descriptions that may, in a sense, cost him his individuality is similar to the psychology of the stammerer. As well as being a speculative thinker, Darwin also had a stammer.[17] He could accurately describe the psychology of the stammerer, in an earlier section of *Zoonomia*; but he could not cure himself (possibly for that very reason: he knew the comprehensive description):

> On this circumstance [trying too hard] depends the impediment of speech before mentioned; the first syllable of a word is causable by volition, but the remainder of it is in common conversation introduced by its association with this first syllable acquired by long habit. Hence when the mind of the stammerer is vehemently employed on some idea of ambition of shining, or fear of not succeeding, the associations of the motions of the muscles of articulation with each other become dissevered by this greater exertion, and he endeavours in vain by voluntary efforts to rejoin the broken association.[18]

The stammerer cannot relax and let himself stammer, in which case he might improve. He has to try, quite humanly, not to stammer; and the effort makes him stammer. Similarly, in the explanation of phenomena, it is perhaps better to relax and to try a few things at a time as modern science does, rather than to try too hard to invent comprehensive models, which will necessarily be mechanical. But the human speculator is, of course, human, and so he must use models, just as the stammerer wants to shine. Thus, Darwin's longest book of the most comprehensive models, animal motion and generation, is provocative, thrilling, and at the same time valiantly comic in its attempt to be comprehensive.

II Phytologia *(1800)*

His other lengthy prose work on natural philosophy, *Phytologia*, actually contains the insight that could, and for the Romantics did, solve the dilemma of the relationship between the mechanical and the organic. Darwin's comic tone is, in part, a response to the futility of trying to give mechanical explanations to organic phenomena. (Part of the tone, of course, simply comes from the human refusal to accept the inhuman nature of the phenomena themselves.) But the definition of human nature is an ever changing concept, and what happened during the eighteenth century was a gradual accommodation of the notion of humanness to the notion of flowing, organic growth. Darwin could not accept this new notion of humanness, but he did describe and explore the metaphor upon which it was based. Philip Ritterbush points out the relation of Darwin's poems to this growing Romantic view of human capabilities:

The creative power of the imagination was symbolized by the growing plant; the critic and historian Meyer Abrams has called this the theory of vegetable genius [in *The Mirror and the Lamp* (1953)]. It probably originated from the belief . . . that plants enjoyed sensation, feeling, and other attributes of animal life. This exaggerated estimate of the faculties of plants was very widespread in the eighteenth century. It is perhaps most strikingly set forth in the extravagant speculative poems of Erasmus Darwin (1731–1802), wherein plants were personified as passionate lovers and endowed with all the powers of animals.[19]

It is, however, Darwin's *Phytologia*, his treatise on vegetable life, that develops this speculative idea most completely in large prose. The analogy of vegetable life to animal life was not a new idea by the time this treatise was published; as Ritterbush suggests, the analogy was not even new to Darwin's writing. In fact, the Lockean-materialistic mode of thinking, which played such an important role in Darwin's career as in that of the entire century, was bound to explore such an analogy since life, as well as nonlife, was assumed to be of a piece. In the middle of the century, David Hartley wrote: "Animals are . . . analogous to Vegetables in many things, and Vegetables to Minerals: So that there seems to be perpetual Thread of Analogy continued from the most perfect Animal to the most imperfect Mineral, even till we come to elementary Bodies themselves."[20]

In the notes to *The Botanic Garden* and then in *Zoonomia*, Darwin again and again picks up this analogy and elaborates it:

Thus, besides a kind of taste at the extremities of their roots, similar to that of the extremities of our lacteal vessels, for the purpose of selecting their proper food . . . vegetable life seems to possess an organ of sense to distinguish the variations of heat, another to distinguish the varying degrees of moisture, another of light, another of touch, and probably another analogous to our sense of smell. To these must be added the indubitable evidence of their passion of love, and I think we may truly conclude, that they are furnished with a common sensorium belonging to each bud, and that they must occasionally repeat those perceptions either in their dreams or waking hours, and consequently possess ideas of so many of the properties of the external world, and of their own existence.[21]

The beauty of Darwin's treatment of the analogy is his absurd attempt to spell it out in carefully elaborated mechanical detail, and it is in the *Phytologia* where he attempts to do so most systematically. In other words, Darwin makes his usual "comic" attempt to save humanity and systematic science from the implications of their own discoveries; and the overall literary effect is one of committed yet playful human energy. Darwin wants to go as far as he can with careful, systematic description; but the further he goes, the more intimation there is that the thing he is describing defies system. And yet he does not surrender; he tries to maintain his "human" rationality even in the face of mystery. One result would be the comic tension between his verse and his ideas, as we have seen and will see in the poems. Another result is this second long treatise on nature that is filled with cheerful contradiction and impossible speculation in large prose.

Like all Darwin's books, even his books of poems, the *Phytologia* is almost like a notebook, a collection of "some" of his speculations and inventions; and this one has appended to it an illustrated description of a method for draining marshes. The book begins with a statement of his systematic purpose:

Agriculture and Gardening, though of such great utility in producing the nutriment of mankind, continue to be only Arts, consisting of numerous detached facts and vague opinions, without a true theory to connect them, or to appreciate their analogy; at a time when many parts of knowledge of much inferior consequence have been nicely arranged, and digested into Sciences.

Our imperfect acquaintance with the physiology and economy of vegetation is the principal cause of the great immaturity of our knowledge of agriculture, and Gardening. I shall therefore first attempt a theory of vegetation. . . .[22]

But before very long his theory is far beyond what can be treated conclusively, and he is attempting to locate the brain of individual plants. He suggests that each bud on a plant is a separate individual with its own brain: "Now as the internal pith of a bud appears to contain or produce the living principle, like the brain and medulla oblongata, or spinal marrow of animals, we have from hence a certain criterion to distinguish one bud from another, or the parent bud from the numerous budlets, which are its offspring, as *there is no communication of the internal pith between them.*"[23]

Another analogy that he explores in some detail is the similarity between the animal fetus and the plant seed or bulb. The images of curving shells and buds in the following passage recall all those bursting curves in the lyric description of birth that appears at the end of "The Economy of Vegetation," one which I quoted at the end of the previous chapter:

This analogy between the vegetable and animal fetus in respect to their production, nourishment, and oxygenation, is as forcible in so obscure a subject, as it is curious; and may in large buds, as of the horse-chestnut, be almost seen by the naked eye. If with a pen-knife the remaining rudiment of the last year's leaf, and of the new bud in its bosom, be cut away slice by slice, the seven ribs of the last year's leaf will be seen to have arisen from the pith in seven distinct points, making a curve; and the new bud to have been produced in their center, and to have pierced the alburnum and bark, and grown without the assistance of a mother.[24]

Throughout his writings, Darwin continually expresses awe at the fecundity of nature; but in his exploration of plant life he finds a phenomenon of greater fecundity than in anything in animal life. Alluded to in the quotation above, it is a kind of hermaphroditism whereby plants send out shoots, or, in Darwin's terms, actually reproduce themselves from any point on their surface: "Nothing known in the animal world resembles this universality of the generative faculty throughout almost the whole of an individual vegetable being, except the number of new polypi said to arise at the same time from different parts of the same individual animal."[25] He labels this phenomenon "lateral reproduction", distinguishes it slightly from hermaphroditism in which both sexes are in one individual, and says that it "forms an exception to the general axiom of the great Harvey, 'all things from eggs.'"[26]

The awesomeness of nature's fecundity, however, is actually perfected, according to Darwin, in the process of sexual reproduction rather than in lateral reproduction. Although the simpler mode of reproduction may seem to exhibit more power, the carefully channeled nature of sexual reproduction introduces greater variety (in fact, infinite variety over time) in the product: "And at the same time it must be observed, that the sexual reproduction is the chef d'ouvre, the master-piece of nature, as by the paternal or lateral reproduction by the same species only are propagated ad infinitium; whereas by the sexual mode of reproduction a countless variety of animals are introduced into the world, and much pleasure is afforded to those which already exist in it."[27]

The notion of "pleasure" is a fine example of Darwin's distorting his insights with the use of analogy: because he needs to distort in order to "save" the wonderfully fecund, randomness of nature and to make it seem human, he argues that all sexual reproduction involves pleasure for the parents. This pleasure is part of the basis for the personifications in "The Loves of the Plants," but in *Phytologia* it keeps Darwin speculating about what organs of perception there might be in plants to experience this pleasure:

Lastly, in many flowers the anthers when mature approach the stigma, in others the female organ approaches to the male. I ask, by what means are the anthers in many flowers, and stigmas in other flowers, directed to find their paramours? Is this curious kind of storge [natural affection] produced my mechanic attraction, or by the sensation of love? The latter opinion is supported by the strongest analogy, because a reproduction of the species is the consequence; and then another organ of sense must be wanted to direct these vegetable amourettes to find each other; one probably analogous to our sense of smell which in the animal world directs the newborn infant to its source of nourishment; and in some animals directs the male to the female; and they may thus possess a faculty of perceiving as well as of producing odours.[28]

Darwin's theories in his prose treatises, which are, I think, the basis for his comic acceptance of limits in the poems, tend to go much further than mere descriptions of plant or animal physiology, for he wants ultimately to describe both the fecundity of nature and the human appropriateness of that fecundity. In order to do the latter, he argues by speculative analogy which leads him finally to a recognition of the absurdity in what he is trying to do; and his poems are his expression of that absurdity with their ridiculous personified plant life. Darwin does discover, or at least express well, the truth that was to be basis of Romanticism: that in nature all things are unique and possess a fecund power of growth; they create themselves, wholly themselves, and that is all. In other words, the rational habits of showing similarity and analogy between things in order to say, for instance, that a manly plant is as happy as a manly man have no relevance to the reality of fecund nature.[29]

Possibly there are universal forces, but there is no indication that they are human. But we are men, of course; or, more to the point, Darwin was a man; therefore, he continually tried to apply human analogy to what he sensed was only teeming phenomena.

A section near the end of *Phytologia* is entitled "The Happiness of Organic Life," and it can serve as a final illustration from this treatise of Darwin's dilemma. His line of argument in the section is that throughout the various activities in nature, such as the struggle and survival of the fittest and the digestion of plants by animals, there is a kind of arithmetic increase of happiness that continually increases. For example, there is pleasure attendant upon a plant's transformation of matter into food: "The vascular actions of vegetables, which perform their digestion, sanguification, and secretion, convert the elements of air and water, or other aliments, which they receive from organized matter decomposing beneath the soil, into more compounded or more solid materials, as into vegetable vessels, muscles, membranes, nerves, and ligneous fibres; and a degree of pleasurable sensation must be supposed from the strongest analogy to attend this activity of their systems."[30]

Then there is more pleasure when an animal eats the plant. In the middle of this section, however, Darwin interrupts his personification of all phenomena to include several paragraphs written, he says, by "A philosopher, whom I left in my library, [and who] has perused the above paragraphs."[31] That philosopher seems actually to be Darwin himself, and what he does is make fun of his own attempt to explain by analogy that happiness prevails in nature. In other words, Darwin knows that his vision is beginning to uncover a kind of inhuman fecundity in things, so he mocks himself for being more sanguine. Yet, at the same time, his commitment to the older notion of human nature requires that he end this section with the following impossible bit of rhetoric (arguing that that nonliving sedimentary droppings are records of past happiness): "We hence acquire this sublime and interesting idea; that all the calcareous mountains in the world, and all the strata of clay, coal, marl, sand and iron, which are incumbent on them, are MONUMENTS OF THE PAST FELICITY OF ORGANIZED NATURE! AND CONSEQUENTLY OF THE BENEVOLENCE OF THE DEITY!"[32]

In short, Darwin chooses to personify and to describe by analogy to man all organic matter, and even inorganic matter in places. But, in fact, he is describing a monistic materialism and disguising it as human. And he might just as well have turned the analogy around and described all organic life in terms of material forces—which is actually what analogy, being a mechanical figure of speech, does.

III *Miscellaneous Prose*

Near the end of *Phytologia*, Darwin prints two of his short, occasional poems: "Address to Swilcar Oak" and "The Cultivation of Brocoli."[33] The first poem consists of thirteen couplets; the second is about twice as long. The technique in both is similar to that in the longer poems, while the subject is also the same: everyday reality is personified and made glossy. Throughout his long life, Darwin wrote occasional poems on subjects like learning shorthand or how to make a vase; and now and then historians discover a new one.[35] Similarly, his career was full of miscellaneous prose composition, a collection almost too various to describe. He wrote prose notes to each of his long poems, and then he wrote "Additional Notes" that amount to short essays and printed them at the end of each long poem. The note on the Portland vase at the end of "The Economy of Vegetation" is an essay on art criticism and the Eleusinian mysteries, which I quoted from in Chapter 1. The note on reproduction at the end of *The Temple of Nature* is a beautifully written repetition of his ideas on generation and evolution as he had explained them earlier in *Zoonomia* and *Phytologia*. He wrote prose interludes separating the cantos of "The Loves of the Plants," and in those he used a dialogue form between "Poet" and "Bookseller." The most interesting dialogue is in the third interlude in which prosody is discussed; Darwin invents a wonderfully theoretical method of scansion that is impractical for scanning any verse but which at least allows him to experiment a bit with trisyllabic substitutions.[35] Finally, sandwiched between *Zoonomia* and *Phytologia*, he published a short book on education entitled, *A Plan for the Conduct of Female Education in Boarding Schools* (1797).

This tract on education was written as advice for his two illegitimate daughters, the "Misses Parker," when they were establishing a boarding school in the town of Ashburne.[36] Darwin's generally tough-minded, almost cynical view of the way things are can be seen, however, in the advice he gives for this specific purpose. In talking about the kind of "polite literature" to use in the school, he is suspicious of novels and even of poetry that gives a sentimental view and distorts the misery in life:

> no real harm could probably arise from their seeing human nature in all the classes of life, not only as it should be, or as it may be imagined to be, but as it really exists, since without comparison there can be no judgment, and consequently no real knowledge.
> It must nevertheless be observed, that the excessive study of novels is universally an ill employment at any time of life; not only because such readers are liable to acquire a romantic taste; and to return from the flowery scenes of fiction to the common duties of life with a degree of regret; but because the highwrought scenes of elegant distress display'd in novels have been found to blunt the feelings of such readers towards real objects of misery. . . . The works of the poets, as well as those of the writers of novels, require to be selected with great caution.[37]

The sense here of his dislike for flowery literature suggests that he must have thought he was not giving just flowery literature in his poems. Thus, I argue throughout this book that the comic effect is his overall literary effect. Furthermore, Darwin's basic distrust is deeper than a mere distrust of sentimental literature, and he advises that young ladies be made shrewd judges of character, not apt to be fooled by appearances (as we must not be fooled by appearances in his writing): "This knowledge of physiognomy, which is perhaps only to be acquired at schools, by giving a promptitude of understanding the present approbation or dislike, and the good or bad designs, of those whom we converse with, becomes of hourly use in almost every department of life."[38] In fact, Darwin's writing on education contains all of the elements of Darwin the comic manipulator because the purpose of the comic attitude is to survive and to build, which, of course, is the purpose of education. So, even though there is much misery and chaos in the world, tentative order, tentative analogy, can be established. In his section on "Fortitude," Darwin recommends for ladies what is really his own strongest weapon (humor is a variation) throughout his writing, and presumably his life: "But that serene strength of mind, which faces unavoidable danger with open eyes, prepared to counteract or to bear the necessary evils of life, is equally valuable as a male or female acquisition. This is term'd presence of mind; it depends on our judgment of the real value of things; and on our application of those causes, which contribute to turn disagreeable circumstances to the best advantage; and can therefore only be acquired by the general cultivation of good sense and of knowledge."[39]

One of Darwin's means of turning "disagreeable circumstances to the best advantage" was to invent theories and analogies which he knew all too well to be merely tentative. But also simply writing itself was a means; for much of his writing, especially his prose, had some of the characteristics of a journal since, throughout his various notes and books, references like the following are found: "On observing a Canary bird this morning, January 28, 1772, at the house of Mr. Harvey, near Tutbury, in Derbyshire. . . ."[40] Many years later he still writes with the same sense of immediacy: "Early this morning, June 18, 1798, observed a remarkable honey-dew on an extensive row of nut-trees, corylus avellana, which grow by the side of a pond of water. . . ."[41] He knew the real value of things, and he recorded as he saw and experienced them; but he also knew and had a profound vision of the randomness and chaos of things. Thus, he played continually with analogies, and he not only reports what he saw on a particular day but also explores a theory to relate it to other things.

The "largeness" of his prose comes primarily from his continual effort to express these theories adequately. And in his prose works, at least, he goes straight on in a direct approach trying to find words for his vision of an infinitely complex materialism. The etymology of the word "prose" suggests that it is that use of language that goes straight on, whereas "verse" is language that turns.[42] I suggest that Darwin's discovery of, and more or less effective expression of, his vision of vast organic horizons necessitated the "turnings" of his verse as a comic defense against the implications of the vision. But the prose does not "turn" on itself much. Now and then the reader laughs at the wonderful absurdity of the far-reaching vision, but Darwin does not call for these laughs as he does more consciously with the rhetoric of the couplet. Perhaps there is something inherently comic in Darwin's entire vision. But the prose, at least, exhibits straightforward largeness as its prime characteristic.

One final example illustrates the awe that his prose can generate for the most gruesome and inhuman phenomena. His vision is, in a sense, simply a vision of the sheer energy and fecundity of life, of which human life is only one small segment. He tries, of course, to tame this energy by the use of analogy and to keep it within civilized proportions by the use of comic devices. But often, especially in his prose, the energy is seen in its raw power. The quotation, from the "Additional Notes" at the end of *The Temple of Nature*, begins by describing with awe the energy that the smallpox virus possesses; then it describes the reproductive energy that the insect larva seems to possess; and, finally, the passage praises the Creator of it all, but almost as an afterthought. Or, more logically, He *was* the original catalyst; but the proliferating energy seems to have left Him far behind:

There is one curious circumstance of animal life analogous in some degree to this wonderful power of reproduction; which is seen in the propagation of some contagious diseases. Thus one grain of variolous matter, inserted by inoculation, shall in about seven days stimulate the system into unnatural action; which in about seven days more produces ten thousand times the quantity of a similar material thrown out on the skin in pustules!

The mystery of reproduction, which alone distinguished organic life from mechanic or chemic action, is yet wrapt in darkness. During the decomposition of organic bodies, where there exists a due degree of warmth with moisture, new microscopic animals of the most minute kind are produced; and these possess the wonderful power of reproduction, or of producing animals similar to themselves in their general structure, but with frequent additional improvements; which the preceding parent might in some measure have acquired by his habits of life or accidental situation.

But it may appear too bold in the present state of our knowledge on this subject, to suppose that all vegetables and animals now existing were originally derived from the smallest microscopic ones, formed by spontaneous vitality? and that they have by innumerable reproductions, during innumerable centuries of time, gradually acquired the size, strength, and excellence of form and faculties, which they now possess? and that such amazing powers were originally impressed on matter and spirit by the great Parent of Parents! Cause of Causes! Ens Entium![43]

Darwin's rhetoric in the final paragraph is significant. He says his vision may be too bold, and he repeats the catch phrases of piety toward the Creator that appear again and again in his passages on this theme. But the overall impression of his repeated treatment of this topic of generation (the title of the note above is "Reproduction") is that the statement is not too bold. He may not be able to prove a theory of materialistic evolution over vast time, but he has the vision.

CHAPTER 4
The Temple of Nature *(1803)*

EVEN though Darwin's vision of the nature of physical reality may anticipate much in the scientific thinking that was to come after him, his interest and fame as a writer must rest on his decision to "round things off" with heroic couplets. His prose works are significant (and fun), but more significant is the fact that he chose to be comic and to be ornamental. As I have continually suggested, these literary effects are deliberate and intentional—not accidental. For example, even in the epigraph to his most ambitious prose work, *Zoonomia*, we can find his characteristic couplet rhetoric: circular structures and images of circles combined with overblown personification that gives a slightly clumsy, comic, Falstaffian cast to whatever is being imaged. The epigraph is Darwin's translation of the famous passage from the *Aeneid* in which Anchises begins his speech to Aeneas revealing the "mysteries" of nature. Thus, it is appropriate to quote it both as a reminder that the heroic couplet rhetoric is much a part of Darwin's writing, even prefacing his major prose work, and as a transition into the discussion of Darwin's own last attempt to reveal the mysteries of nature:

> *Earth, on whose lap a thousand nations tread,*
> *And Ocean, brooding his prolific bed,*
> *Night's changeful orb, blue pole, and silvery zones,*
> *Where other worlds encircle other suns,*
> *One mind inhabits, one diffusive soul*
> *Wields the large limbs, and mingles with the whole.* [1]

The images for personified nature in *The Temple of Nature* abound in this same excessive concreteness (the "large limbs" of the universe), so that "Nature," either male or female as we shall see, becomes both human and funny. But this last long poem of Darwin's is, in a sense, not his best, although his characteristic themes and comic devices stand out clearly in the poem. Robert E. Schofield says it is a "tired book" with "little of the verbal polish and brilliant imagery which help excuse the poetic defects of the *Botanic Garden*." [2] In other words, we do not find in *The Temple of Nature* teeming high points, such as the passage celebrating birth at the end of "The

Economy of Vegetation"; but we do find a competent, final statement of Darwin's comic "mystery religion" with its central themes
and devices.

The poem is divided into four cantos, as were the other two long
poems. The speaker begins as the poet, but he soon blends into a
strange identity with "the muse" herself. The structure of the poem,
then, is simply that the muse is led through the Temple of Nature by
a Hierophant, or Priestess, who is sometimes identified as Urania;
in other words, the muse is gradually initiated into the mysteries of
the Temple. This initiation follows a systematic progression that
allows for the canto divisions of the poem. In Canto I, the Hierophant tells about the origin of life from microscopic chunks of
matter beneath the sea. Canto II deals with the methods of reproduc-
ing life with a celebration of sexual reproduction as the most
advanced method. Canto III initiates the muse into the details of
human psychology, following the categories from *Zoonomia* of the
four subdivisions of animal motion. Finally, Canto IV, entitled
"Of Good and Evil," explains the role of death in the evolutionary
progress of life and tries to justify a teeming nature in which there
is plenty of individual loss. After all this explanation, the Hierophant
is able to unveil for the initiate muse the Goddess of Nature who
presides over the Temple; and the poem ends.

I *The Theme of Marriage*

Darwin uses various techniques throughout his verse to make
his characters as sensuous and as "sexual" as possible.[3] In *The
Temple of Nature*, one of the fully developed allegorical figures
is the Hierophant, or priestess, of the Temple. (The Botanic
Goddess in the earlier poems is a sketchier, less-developed
figure visually, although she represents something quite similar.)
The Goddess of Nature herself is shrouded in mystery,
and we see little of her femininity, which is actually rather grotesque:
"Tower upon tower her beamy forehead crests, And births unnumber'd milk her hundred breasts."[4] By contrast, her priestess is very
beautiful—a sensuous prototype for all of the beautiful women
Darwin describes, from the simplest personified plant to the several
accounts of the mythological Venus.

The description of the priestess takes over a hundred lines in the
first canto of *The Temple of Nature*, and she appears richly abundant

in visual detail. Her dress is regal and colorful (more like a human queen with no mention of the hundred breasts). The last six lines in the description include references to bright colors and fine materials as well as to her white skin and shapely body:

> *Bright chains of pearl, with golden buckles brac'd.*
> *Clasp her white neck, and zone her slender waist;*
> *Thin folds of silk in soft meanders wind*
> *Down her fine form, and undulate behind;*
> *The purple border, on the pavement roll'd,*
> *Swells in the gale, and spreads its fringe of gold.* [5]

It is not merely individual figures, but "immortal love" in general as the prime generative force that is described again and again in Darwin's verse. And the couplets that deal with this important theme are often the most interesting in the use of expressive devices. For example, a couplet near the beginning of Canto I of this poem is an outstanding use of the complex pattern of chiastic rhyme in which the preceding words complicate and add to the pattern. The poet invokes love, and the patterns in the couplet suggest why it is so important:

> $\quad\quad\quad\quad\quad\quad\quad$ A $\quad\quad$ B
> *You! whose wide arms, in soft embraces hurl'd*
> $\quad\quad\quad\quad\quad\quad$ B $\quad\quad$ A
> *Round the vast frame, connect the whirling world.* [6]

The chiastic effect is between the two verbs (B), which seem to go together, and the nouns (A), which carry the sense of the couplet: that love embraces the world. The sense of the verbs is more active than that of the nouns while at the same time the verbs represent two aspects of the same action: the vigorous circular motion of the whirling world and the milder circular motion of "soft embraces." The accidental sound resemblances of the rhyme, the additional alliterative sound resemblance of the verbs, and the chiastic effect by which the sense goes back and forth between softness and vigor— all of these relationships bind the couplet together into an intricate pattern of sound and sense.

Such patterns are used expressively to convey the importance of the sexual love which Darwin believes to be the most highly developed kind of love. His admiration for this accomplishment of Nature helps to explain the frequency of images of sex and marriage in his poems. (We recall the discussion of erotic happiness and marriage as images for comic compromise in Chapter 1.) In the second

canto of *The Temple of Nature*, he gives the fullest poetic treatment
to this theme, and its treatment is characteristically mixed: serious,
sensuous, mythic, as well as comic. In the first half of the canto,
before the "Deities of Sexual Love" have actually arrived (they
arrive in 1. 244), the priestess tells of the creation of Eve; and
Darwin uses visual imagery, assonance, and alliteration in order
to make a seriously sensuous passage:

> *Down her white neck and o'er her bosom roll'd,*
> *Flow'd in sweet negligence her locks of gold;*
> *Round her fine form the dim transparence play'd,*
> *And show'd the beauties, that it seem'd to shade.*
> *—Enamour'd* ADAM *gaz'd with fond surprise,*
> *And drank delicious passion from her eyes;*
> *Felt the new thrill of young Desire, and press'd*
> *The graceful Virgin to his glowing breast.—*
> *The conscious Fair betrays her soft alarms,*
> *Sinks with warm blush into his closing arms,*
> *Yields to his fond caress with wanton play,*
> *And sweet, reluctant, amorous, delay.*[7]

Darwin was apparently so eager to achieve a rich, sensuous texture
in this description of Adam and Eve that he borrowed from Milton's
Book IV of *Paradise Lost* line 331 which is quoted verbatim in
the last couplet above. The borrowed line is, of course, good
expressive sound; but the credit must be given to Milton. The rhyme
that Darwin contributes, however, is a good metaphoric one because
it underlines the fact that "wanton play" is based to a great extent on
delaying.

But, when he begins to describe the advantages of reproduction
by sexual love, with all its potential for variousness and evolutionary
change, he lapses regularly into the tone of comic absurdity. This
tone, of course, had been the main characteristic of "The Loves of
the Plants," but in this later poem similar reasons for the tone, as
well as devices for achieving it, can be seen. Sexual love, the source
of variousness in nature, implies the continuing, fluxing change
that Darwin saw so well and that seems so threatening to human
uniqueness. Darwin's solution both for describing this nonhuman
phenimena and for building a comic defense against it is to personify
and to burlesque, as well as to image the compromise of merriage:

Hence on green leaves the sexual Pleasures dwell,
And Loves and Beauties crowd the blossom's bell;
The wakeful Anther in his silken bed
O'er the pleased Stigma bows his waxen head;
With meeting lips and mingling smiles they sup
Ambrosial dewdrops from the nectar'd cup;
Or buoy'd in air the plumy Lover springs,
And seeks his panting bride on Hymen-wings
  The Stamen males, with appetencies just,
Produce a formative prolific dust;
With apt propensities, the Styles recluse
Secrete a formative prolific juice;
These in the pericarp erewhile arrive,
Rush to each other, and embrace alive.
—Form'd by new powers progressive parts succeed,
Join in one whole, and swell into a seed.[8]

Throughout Darwin's writing, the marriage of opposite sexes and the resulting generation are important themes; and, despite the frequent burlesque tone (or perhaps because of it), we know that he takes sexual love and marriage very seriously. Also, as I have explained in Chapter 1, marriage is a symbol for the comic compromise itself—something that is imperfect, yet stubbornly maintained. Thus, *The Temple of Nature* ends with a ceremony in which the muse, who has listened for four cantos to the Hierophant explain the mysteries of the Temple, ascends the altar; withdraws the veil from the Goddess of Nature, whose overseeing presence has been sensed in the Temple since the description in Canto I of her hundred breasted splendor; kneels; and "Lifts her ecstatic eyes to Truth Divine."[9] This ceremony is a religious one certainly, the final initiation in the mystery religion; but it is also suggestive of a marriage ceremony with the altar, the veil, and the solemn seriousness. A note of Darwin's characteristic burlesque tone appears in his treatment of the two "virgin Sisters," the muse and the Hierophant, in the systematic progress toward the Goddess[10] because of the grotesque description of the Goddess, as well as because of hints of the hermaphroditic qualities of the girls. But, compared to the ending of "The Loves of the Plants," these relationships at the end of *The Temple of Nature* end in a solemn marriage. Thus the theme in Darwin's poems of love relationships or marriage is finally treated solemnly and, significantly, almost without reference to sexual play.

II   *The Theme of Metamorphosis or Hermaphroditism*

The fact that the three characters in *The Temple of Nature*—the muse, the Hierophant, and the Goddess—are all female and that the poem ends with the hint of a marriage ceremony is interesting because it raises the possibility of hermaphroditism, which would, in turn, be a continuation of the theme of metamorphosis that runs throughout Darwin's writing. Just as many of the plants in "The Loves of the Plants" are hermaphrodites, perhaps the "virgin Sisters" are, and certainly the Goddess of Nature should be. Nature itself is hermaphroditic, and several times in the poem nature is referred to in the masculine, "Nature's Lord."[11] Another piece of evidence for the possibility of an implied sexual metamorphosis within the characters of this poem is Darwin's fascination with the topic in his prose notes to his various poems. We have already seen from his note on the Portland vase in "The Economy of Vegetation"[12] that he understood the Hierophant in the Eleusinian mysteries to have been bisexual. His note on hermaphroditism in this poem purports to reject it as an inferior type of sexuality and is part of his statement of the idea of progress and the superiority of sexual love. But, just as Irwin Primer argues that Darwin believes equally, and possibly even more strongly, in the continual recurrence of eternal verities in nature,[13] I suggest that his belief in sexual progress does not rule out a fascination with hermaphroditism, which seems to be present in the following note, along with paean to progress at the end of the note:

The arguments which have been adduced to show, that mankind and quadrupeds were formerly in an hermaphrodite state, are first deduced from the present existence of breasts and nipples in all the males; which latter swell on titillation like those of the females, and which are said to contain a milky fluid at their birth; and it is affirmed, that some men have given milk to their children in desert countries, where the mother has perished; as the male pigeon is said to give a kind of milk from his stomach along with the regurgitated food, to the young doves. . . .

It has been supposed by some, that mankind were formerly quadrupeds as well as hermaphrodites. . . .

Perhaps all the productions of nature are in their progress to greater perfection! an idea countenanced by modern discoveries and deductions concerning the progressive formation of the terraqueous globe, and consonant to the dignity of the Creator of all things.[14]

Finally, in support of Darwin's expression in this poem of hermaphroditism, which would be a variation of his theme of metamorphosis, it is significant that his speakers are all female, whereas much of what they say is made up of Darwin's own opinions and sentiments. This detail of the poem is also consistent with his strategy of double-truth or evasiveness. The most personal sentiment in the poem is the muse's first-person lament over death, which comes after she has been describing death in general; she says:

> *And now, e'en I, whose verse reluctant sings*
> *The changeful state of sublunary things,*
> *Bend o'er Mortality with silent sighs,*
> *And wipe the secret tear-drops from my eyes,*
> *Hear through the night one universal groan,*
> *And mourn unseen for evils not my own,*
> *With restless limbs and throbbing heart complain,*
> *Stretch'd on the rack of sentimental pain!*[15]

And even though the muse qualifies her grief in the above passage by saying it is universal, she is not convincing; for the passage seems to me a reference to something personal, possibly Darwin's own grief since the suicide of his second son in 1799 saddened Darwin deeply.[16] If this passage is personal, this is just another evidence that he transforms himself into a female speaker partly in order to support the strategy of evasiveness and to express the notion of hermaphroditism. Also, of course, the muse as the initiate into the mysteries of nature would be likely to be Darwin himself, the poet and the inquisitive scientist.

Darwin's vision of change, or mutability, as he images it with the themes of metamorphosis and hermaphroditism, is both teeming with life and unsettling. The vision is the reason, of course, for his continual desire for comic marriage, his belief in the "progress" of sexual love; and it is also closely linked to his third theme of "circling" or circularity. For example, both the muse's lament in Canto IV about the ravages of time and Urania's answer contain beautiful descriptions of metamorphosis. As the following quotations indicate—the muse's lament from early in the canto, and part of the answer of the priestess—the arrangement of the lines and half-lines in the first passage suggests an intricate circling while the sense of both passages is the metamorphosis or subsuming of all things into all other things:

> *The wolf, escorted by his milk-drawn dam,*
> *Unknown to mercy, tears the guiltless lamb;*
> *The towering eagle, darting from above,*
> *Unfeeling rends the inoffensive dove;*
> *The lamb and dove on living nature feed,*
> *Crop the young herb, or crush the embryon seed.*
> *Nor spares the loud owl in her dusky flight,*
> *Smit with sweet notes, the minstrel of the night;*
> *Nor spares, enamour'd of his radiant form,*
> *The hungry nightingale the glowing worm;*
> *Who with bright lamp alarms the midnight hour,*
> *Climbs the green stem, and slays the sleeping flower. . . .*

> *Hence when a Monarch or a mushroom dies,*
> *Awhile extinct the organic matter lies;*
> *But, as a few short hours or years revolve,*
> *Alchemic powers the changing mass dissolve;*
> *Born to new life unnumber'd insects pant,*
> *New buds surround the microscopic plant;*
> *Whose embryon senses, and unwearied frames,*
> *Feel finer goads, and blush with purer flames;*
> *Renascent joys from irritation spring,*
> *Stretch the long root, or wave the aurelian wing.*
> *When thus a squadron or an army yields,*
> *And festering carnage loads the waves or fields;*
> *When few from famines or from plagues survive,*
> *Or earthquakes swallow half a realm alive;—*
> *While Nature sinks in Time's destructive storms,*
> *The wrecks of Death are but a change of forms;*
> *Emerging matter from the grave returns,*
> *Feels new desires, with new sensations burns;*
> *With youth's first bloom a finer sense acquires,*
> *And Loves and Pleasures fan the rising fires.*[17]

We are familiar enough now with Darwin's technique to recognize how the implications of "the facts" above elicit from him the comic personifications about love in order to make the facts more humanly manageable. But Darwin's comic tone is not a sentimental obliteration of reality; it is his way of looking at reality and not being destroyed by it.

III   *The Theme of Circularity*

What the initiate discovers, as the priestess helps her "look at" reality, is not entirely linear progress but partly the regeneration cycle mentioned above and partly something like a balance in nature whereby death complements life in a continually circling pattern. In this poem, the discovery is made in a specific place, the Temple. This conception of a locale can be used to help clarify Darwin's overall frame story of a modern-day mystery religion. And this place embodies in its very architecture the pattern of circularity:

> *Here, high in air, unconscious of the storm,*
> *Thy temple, Nature, rears its mystic form;*
> *From earth to heaven, unwrought by mortal toil,*
> *Towers the vast fabric on the desert soil;*
> *O'er many a league the ponderous domes extend,*
> *And deep in the earth the ribbed vaults descend;*
> *A thousand jasper steps with circling sweep;*
> *Lead the slow votary up the winding steep;*
> *Ten thousand piers, now join'd and now aloof,*
> *Bear on their branching arms the fretted roof.*
>
> *Here o'er piazza'd courts, and long arcades,*
> *The bowers of Pleasure root their waving shades;*
> *Shed o'er the pansied moss a checker'd gloom,*
> *Bend with new fruits, with flow'rs successive bloom.*
> *Pleased, their light limbs on beds of roses press'd,*
> *In slight undress recumbent beauties rest;*
> *On tiptoe steps surrounding Graces move,*
> *And gay Desires expand their wings above.*[18]

The first part of this description creates the image of a huge dust or storm cloud over the desert, which recalls the passages on the water cycle in "The Economy of Vegetation," but the second part of the description adds the element of sensuous sexual pleasure to this allegorical picture of the "locale" of nature.

The invocation to this poem also shows us the image of circularity interwoven with the notion of love. I quote the first couplet of the poem, and then skip to the invocation of love:

> *By firm immutable immortal laws*
>
> *Impress'd on Nature by the Great First Cause,*
> *Say, Muse! . . .*

> *Immortal Love! who ere the morn of Time,*
> *On wings outstretch'd, o'er Chaos hung sublime*
> *Warm'd into life the bursting egg of Night,*
> *And gave young Nature to admiring Light!*
> *You! whose wide arms, in soft embraces hurl'd*
> *Round the vast frame, connect the whirling world!*
> *Whether immersed in day, the Sun your throne,*
> *You gird the planets in your silver zone;*
> *Or warm, descending on ethereal wing,*
> *The Earth's cold bosom with the beams of spring;*
> *Press drop to drop, to atom atom bind,*
> *Link sex to sex, or rivet mind to mind;*
> *Attend my song!—With rosy lips rehearse,*
> *And with your polish'd arrows write my verse!—*
> *So shall my lines soft-rolling eyes engage,*
> *And snow-white fingers turn the volant page;*
> *The smiles of Beauty all my toils repay,*
> *And youths and virgins chant the living lay.*[19]

As we have seen, the image of "the Egg" associated with the idea of birth is a favorite one of Darwin. I suggest that the circular, or at least curved, egg that is expanding or "bursting" embodies the basic image of circularity representing the fecundity and regeneration of nature. Thus the Temple itself is a kind of bursting egg. Female beauty, from full breasts to the facetiously treated "rolling eyes" in the above passage, is also not only attractive but is associated with vital nature in its circularity. And finally, Darwin's verse because of its circular architecture is also equated with the Temple of a mystery religion.

One explanation of why circularity is so pleasing to him is Darwin's theory from Hogarth about the relationship of beauty to the mother's breast. The verse in this part of *The Temple of Nature* is is not so good as passages expressing circularity already quoted from "The Economy of Vegetation," but the note appended to the verse here is his best expression of the appeal of circularity:

All these various kinds of pleasure at length become associated with the form of the mother's breast; . . . And hence at our maturer years, when any object of vision is presented to us, which by its waving or spiral lines bears any similitude to the form of the female bosom, whether it be found in a landscape with soft gradations of rising and descending surface, or in the forms of some antique vases, or in other works of the pencil or the chisel, we feel a general glow of delight, which seems to influence all our senses; and if the object be not too large, we experience an attraction to embrace it with our arms, and to salute it with our lips, as we did in our early infancy the bosom of our mother. And thus we find, according to the ingenious idea of Hogarth, that the waving lines of beauty were originally taken from the temple of Venus.[20]

In fact, Darwin seems fascinated by the possibility that the spiral or circle represents ideal form throughout nature. This fascination helps to explain his preference for the circular schemes of couplet rhetoric, such as chiasmus, as well as for a kind of strong-stress meter in which two heavy stresses at each end of the line give a circular balance around the weaker stress in the middle. For example, the concept of circling is described, and the meter of the fifth line, at least, does pivot around the weaker stress on the word "of" in the middle:

> Untipt with claws the circling fingers close,
> With rival points the bending thumbs oppose,
> Trace the nice lines of form with sense refined,
> And clear ideas charm the thinking mind.
> Whence the fine organs of the touch impart
> Ideal figure, source of every art;
> Time, motion, number, sunshine or the storm,
> But mark varieties in Nature's form.[21]

As a second example, variations in metrical stress play a significant role because of the sixteen lines in the passage nine have only four strong stresses, suggesting pivotal or circling movement. This passage is the elegant description of the spontaneous generation of life, and the heavy stresses are marked:

> Núrs'd by warm sún-beams in priméval cáves
> Orgánic Life begán benéath the wáves.
> First Héat from chémic dissolútion springs,
> And gíves to mátter its eccéntric wíngs;
> With stróng Repúlsion párts the explóding máss,
> Mélts into lýmph, or kíndles into gás.
> Attráction néxt, as éarth or aír subsídes,
> The pónderous átoms from the líght divídes,
> Appróaching párts with quíck embráce combínes,
> Swells into sphéres, and léngthens into línes.
> Lást, as fine góads the glúten-thréads excíte,

> *Córds grapple córds, and webs with webs uníte;*
> *And quíck Contráction with ethéreal fláme*
> *Líghts into lífe the fíbre-wóven fráme.*
> *Hénce without párent by spontáneous bírth*
> *Ríse the first spécks of ánimated éarth.*[22]

Not only does Darwin's verse have a circular architecture in individual lines and couplets, and not only does the plotting suggest expanding circularity (as was discussed in detail in Chapter 1), but also this poem as a whole ends where it begins. Actually, it is the final speech of the Hierophant before the "marriage" ceremony that ends with the same line that begins the poem. Although Elizabeth Sewell has pointed out this structural nicety, she fails generally to give Darwin enough credit for technical skill elsewhere.[23] Several lines from this conclusion to the Hierophant's last speech permit us to consider finally what her secret is, but it should be noticed that the speech ends exactly as the poem began:

> *Thus the tall mountains, that emboss the lands,*
> *Huge isles of rock, and continents of sands,*
> *Whose dim extent eludes the inquiring sight,*
> *Are mighty Monuments of past Delight;*
> *Shout round the globe, how Reproduction strives*
> *With vanquished Death,—and Happiness survives;*
> *How Life increasing peoples every clime,*
> *And young renascent Nature conquers Time;*
> *—And high in golden characters record*
> *The immense munificence of Nature's Lord!—*
> *   He gives and guides the sun's attractive force,*
> *And steers the planets in their silver course;*
> *With heat and light revives the golden day,*
> *And breathes his spirit on organic clay;*
> *With hand unseen directs the general cause*
> *By firm immutable immortal Laws.*[24]

If the poem is a revelation of the secret in a mystery religion, what, then, is the secret? The easiest answer, of course, is a paraphrase of the lines just quoted: The "immense munificence" of nature must be progress, amelioration; but the secret is less humanly satisfying, more terrifying. We have seen that the dominant images and recurring themes deal primarily with a variety of love relationships, with metamorphosis, and with circular patterns. Within these notions, there is the possibility for birth, regeneration, great fecundity; but nowhere is there the assurance of continuous amelioration. The circular movement of fecund life always returns on itself; it reaches a limit, collapses, and begins over again. This fecundity is the secret of Darwin's mystery religion: the teeming richness of life but ultimately, to use Shelley's phrase, the triumph of life. It is not entirely a pleasant secret because it requires the loss of individual ego. Thus, Darwin conceals the secret by means of his playful tone and with his garish, nearly impenetrable "scenical representations" from all but the most stubborn initiates.

CHAPTER 5

Influence of a Comic Materialist on the Romantics

> Men must endure
> Their going hence, even as their coming hither:
> Ripeness is all.
> —William Shakespeare, *King Lear*

T O endure the triumph of life and to settle for only that is very difficult for bumptious man to do. Most of the brilliant Romantic poets who were growing to maturity when Darwin was publishing his works refused to accept the triumph of life and used all of their inventiveness to redefine human nature sufficiently so that life, as science was revealing it, would not triumph. Darwin's pagan or materialistic pessimism, along with his comic devices for living with this pessimism, played an important role as a kind of negative catalyst for the Romantic movement. He dramatized so well, and so unflinchingly, in his life and in his writings the proliferating variousness of things that only he (and perhaps Lord Byron) could fully face the implications.

Darwin did influence several of the Romantics in certain details of technique, and numerous parallels to his verse can be found in the poets who immediately followed him; in fact, Desmond King-Hele gives a fine concrete listing of passages from each of the Romantics that have a possible indebtedness to Darwin.[1] But Darwin's greatest importance to the writers who followed him was simply his presence. Although he was not revolutionary at all as a writer (unless we grant him a little more art than even I am willing to admit in his skillful fusing of prose, verse, scientific subject matter, and tone), his effect on the Romantic poets was like the effect of the French Revolution: he fascinated and terrified them by showing what could happen if fecund, raw nature is unveiled in her hundred-breasted splendor. For example, Wordsworth incorporated much of the egalitarianism and secularism of the French Revolution into his mature poems at the same time that he rejected the open-endedness, the rationalism, and the Lockean empiricism that encouraged men to manipulate each other in a revolutionary way. The Romantics were driven to make a revolution of the spirit by the terror that accompanied the actual Revolution and its materialism. Darwin helped to drive them and also, like the Revolution, provided some of the ideas that they found and redefined for their own purposes.

The general public made an early and accurate recognition of Darwin's materialism, which it would be worthwhile to notice before explaining the more subtle response and reaction of the poets. As early as 1794 an anonymous poem, entitled *The Golden Age,* appeared that alleged to be "from Erasmus D——n M.D. to Thomas Beddoes M.D."[2] Actually a fierce attack on Darwin and Beddoes, the poem accused them of being Democrats and atheists, but the possibility and demand for such a poem indicates that the consensus was already present in the public mind. Similarly, the parody of Darwin in *The Anti-Jacobin,* entitled "The Loves of the Triangles," which appeared a few years later, indicates that it was easy and fashionable to accuse Darwin of ridiculous speculative flights.[3] Then in 1798 a book-length refutation of *Zoonomia* appeared that contained 560 pages of systematic refutation of each of Darwin's points and that finally condemned him as simply a materialist.[4]

Darwin's stock went steadily down throughout the nineteenth century. Robert Chamberlain has pointed out, for instance, that George Crabbe revised *The Library* in 1807 in order to take from it any resemblance to Darwin's poems. In the original version of the poem in 1781, Crabbe had described the sexual system of plant classification of Linnaeus in a way which Darwin then developed at great length in "The Loves of the Plants." In the revised version, however, Crabbe "cleanses his own passage of its coy sexuality and makes pointed critical references to Darwin's Loves."[5]

Darwin's bad reputation in the press and in the reviews of his works by the end of the century (which, incidentally, severely hurt the reception of *The Temple of Nature*) was, in part, fostered by the fact that even Darwin's friends, or the children of his friends, began to see him as a Jacobin and atheist. Mary Anne Schimmelpenninck, the daughter of Samuel Galton, reports in her *Memoirs* that, when she was a child, the large Doctor Darwin frightened

her not only because of his size but because of his "Jacobinism";
and she then describes the lack of spirituality in his poems: "there
is everything to fix the eye below, on what is transient and mutable;
nothing to raise it above, to the permanent and immutable; there
is all in it to delight the eye or ear, nothing to touch the well-springs
of the heart. It is a beautiful body, delicate, symmetrical, faultless,
but it is destitute of soul."[6]

I *Wordsworth*

In Book XI of *The Prelude*, Wordsworth tells us that he has
turned away from Godwinian rationalism in despair because, to
use the words of Mrs. Schimmelpenninck who was probably
thinking of Wordsworth or his Victorian imitators, it was "destitute of soul." This section is well known, and from it I quote the
ending in the 1850 version:

> *till, demanding formal* proof,
> *And seeking it in every thing, I lost*
> *All feeling of conviction, and, in fine,*
> *Sick, wearied out with contrarieties,*
> *Yielded up moral questions in despair.*
>
> (Bk. XI, 11. 301–5)

Wordsworth goes on in *The Prelude* to describe his rediscovery of
soul—a rediscovery that is verbalized again and again but perhaps
most effectively in the passage that narrates Wordsworth's ascent
of Mount Snowdon:

> *. . . it appeared to me the type*
> *Of a majestic intellect, its acts*
> *And its possessions, what it has and craves,*
> *What in itself it is, and would become.*
> *There I beheld the emblem of a mind*
> *That feeds upon infinity, that broods*
> *Over the dark abyss, intent to hear*
> *Its voices issuing forth to silent light*
> *In one continuous stream; . . .*
> *Such minds are truly from the Deity,*
> *For they are Powers; and hence the highest bliss*
> *That flesh can know is theirs—the consciousness*
> *Of Whom they are, habitually infused*
> *Through every image and through every thought,*
> *And all affections by communion raised*
> *From earth to heaven, from human to divine.*[7]

The significant thing about this description is that it seems to be describing equally well the annihilation of the self, its literal infusion (not just seeing) "into the life of things."[8] Geoffrey Hartman interprets another central passage in *The Prelude* about the sudden rediscovery of self, the Simplon Pass episode, in just this way: what Wordsworth discovers "usurps" the ordinary human self.[9] Northrop Frye, in discussing Thomas Lovell Beddoes, gives the best interpretation, however, of this Romantic discovery of a more organic and profound self, or human nature. Perhaps it is significant that Thomas Lovell Beddoes was the son of the imitator and comic confrere of Darwin, Dr. Thomas Beddoes; for the brittle comic shell of the father may have helped push the son toward the discovery of the ultimate self that Frye describes:

> The feeling that the moment of death is also a crisis of identity is probably as old as human consciousness, and certainly as old as written literature. But it starts out on a new and lonelier journey with the Romantic movement, a journey with a continuous sense that, as Eliot says, the moment of death is every moment, and that absurdity is the only visible form of the meaning of life. It is Beddoes, as far as English literature is concerned, who brings us most directly into contact with the conception of the absurd . . . .[10]

Darwin refuses to confront the dumb center of absurdity that Wordsworth confronts at Simplon Pass and on Mount Snowdon; indeed, Darwin refuses to annihilate his human self in the new definition of human nature that was pending at the turn of the century. (Perhaps it is just that he refuses to lose his life in order to save it.) As a defense, then, Darwin draws a circle of words and myths around that dumb center; and he adopts the facetious tone that nervously keeps talking even though it is not sure of its "self." Darwin, in a manner similar to Godwin, pushed Wordsworth toward his discoveries. And Darwin also contributed, unlike Godwin, the facetious literary tone that he was using as comic defense; but such a tone rankled on the serious Wordsworth: "Depressed, bewildered thus, I did not walk/With scoffers, seeking light and gay revenge/From indiscriminate laughter . . . ."[11]

Actually, Darwin in his scientific writing had made the discovery of the organic self, or the absurd self. He had been unwilling, however, to surrender to it; hence he did not evolve the tone and symbolic imagery that Wordsworth did, perhaps because of his age. Darwin saw into his vision of nature after he had grown to middle age and had become sure of, and comfortable in, a certain civilized notion of self, which he then protected from his vision. Wordsworth, who saw Darwin's vision as a young man, gave himself up to it, at least in his early career. Wordsworth may even have seen it in passages such as the following from *Zoonomia* because we know he used Darwin's treatise for "Goody Blake and Harry Gill"; the passage is Darwin's bland way of discovering that all creatures are probably united in some way: "Owing to the imperfection of language the offspring is termed a *new* animal, but is in truth a branch or elongation of the parent; since a part of the embryon-animal is, or was, a part of the parent; and therefore in strict language it cannot be said to be entirely *new* at the time of its production; and therefore it may retain some of the habits of the parent-system."[12]

Wordsworth, in fact, "perfects" the language of Darwin's passage to the point that he can express through a poetic symbol the "parent-child-system":

> *Hence in a season of calm weather*
> *Though inland far we be,*
> *Our Souls have sight of that immortal sea*
> *Which brought us hither,*
> *Can in a moment travel hither,*
> *And see the Children sport upon the shore,*
> *And hear the mighty waters rolling evermore.*[13]

Darwin's influence is much greater, however, than actual verbal echoes from his writing that may be discovered in Wordsworth, in Coleridge, or in any other Romantic poet; but, although some verbal echoes have been indicated earlier in this book, the nature of Darwin's influence is such that we would actually expect verbal echoes to be minimal. In fact, a clear understanding of the relationship of Darwin to Wordsworth helps us to see in a general, inclusive way the very essence of the Romantic change in literature that, whether or not a direct cause-and-effect influence can be proved (if such a thing can ever be proved), the contiguity of the two is the most instructive fact. Wordsworth's general reaction to Darwin and the notion that his *Preface to Lyrical Ballads, 1800,* was in particular a nervous refutation of Darwin have been noticed by many critics.[14] But Samuel H. Monk in an article on Anna Seward, who was so close to Darwin, pinpoints the major change that Wordsworth helped to bring about: the acceptance of the possibilities of organic growth in poetry. To Professor Monk, the whole Romantic movement flowered once this organic power was unleashed:

> There is never a hint in her writing that she valued a poem for anything beyond its meretricious ornaments or its sentiments. Poetry as a complex structure of language that arranges experience in enduringly true and significant patterns did not occur to her mind. It is inevitable that her view of poetry should have led her to admire Darwin's verses, for they, as well as her own, were the embodiment of her taste. . . .
>
> Miss Seward is useful in reminding us that there was, none the less, a romantic movement: . . . something new was added, as the human mind underwent one of those alterations of structure that periodically have led it to reinterpret the world and the significance of human life. And such a change in the fundamental structure of human perceptions lies behind all the so-called "schools" that literary historians have pointed out to us. . . .
>
> Romantic poetry, when it came full blown, was beyond her ken.[15]

Darwin, unlike Miss Seward, did see the new structure of the mind that was emerging through the study of flowing nature. But he held back from it. And so a difference in tone is the major difference between Wordsworth and Darwin.

II *Coleridge*

The tone of comic defense and holding back, however, is not entirely alien to the Romantic poets; and Darwin's intellectuality, which is nearly synonymous with comic defense, may have had a significant and direct influence on Coleridge. Certainly Coleridge, like Wordsworth, felt the negative influence of what he called "Gaudyverse," and he speaks scornfully of "Darwinizing": "Into this error the author of "The Botanic Garden" has fallen, through the whole of which work, I will venture to assert, there are not twenty images described as a man would describe them in a state of excitement. The poem is written with all the tawdry industry of a milliner anxious to dress up a doll in silks and satins. Dr. Darwin laboured to make his style fine and gaudy, by accumulating and applying all the sonorous and handsome-looking words in our language. This is not poetry. . . . "[16]

In Coleridge's greatest poems, he, of course, never "dresses up" the doll with ornamental artifice. He believes in the organic imagination, and has produced some of the greatest fruits of it. But, at the same time, Coleridge, much more than Wordsworth, emphasizes the frightening unacceptability and the real sublime terror of the imagination. In Coleridge at his best, the discovery of the self in imagination is not just tantamount to death; it is a kind of hell after death as well or, what is worse, an unattainable state. The Ancient Mariner is an obsessed and plagued man; Christabel is haunted, cursed, and/or perverted; but worse than these is the condition of the speakers in "Kubla Khan" and "Dejection: An Ode" who can never achieve the organic imagination and, in fact, fall back on a kind of "gaudiness" even though they desperately want the self-discovery of the organic imagination.

Since there is no question that Coleridge read a great deal of Darwin's prose and verse,[17] I suggest that his wonderfully effective ambivalence toward the imagination is, in part, a more refined version of Darwin's comic tone. The pleasure-done of Xanadu and the domes of the Temple of Nature may be more closely related than has yet been admitted: they both represent unattainable ideals of organic unity.[18] When Darwin was faced with the impossibility and with the absurdity of finding or making one central unity, he compensated by continually making categories and by writing very intellectual treatises and notes—by spiraling out on the periphery of the circle.[19] Coleridge did precisely the same thing in his numerous critical, religious, and political treatises. Coleridge did produce a few wonderful flowers of the organic imagination, but most of the time he "Darwinized." Is that tendency an influence or just a contiguity?

One debt that Coleridge probably owes to Darwin is in literary theory, for Elizabeth Schneider argues very effectively that Coleridge got much of his notion of "dramatic illusion" and "the willing suspension of disbelief" from Darwin: "In his treatment of this whole subject Coleridge is much closer to Darwin than to any other predecessor that I now of. Darwin's ideas were, of course, not wholly original. . . . But a glance at Darwin's most notable predecessors (Kames, Burke, Hartley) serves only to emphasize . . . the extent of his apparent influence on Coleridge."[20]

A few of the most cogent sentences from *Zoonomia* recall Darwin's clear-sighted honesty, or intellectuality. At the end of the passage, Darwin observes that some dramatists must still rely on the "rules" because, presumably, their works do not have the verve or organic unity to stand alone. Strict intellectual analysis must show (as Locke discovered) that nothing can stand alone, short of its death and inclusion with all other things. In addition to giving Coleridge the notion of dramatic illusion, Darwin's writings must have impressed him with the unillusioned despair or "dejection" that strict intellectuality yields:

> So when we are enveloped in deep contemplation of any kind, or in reverie, as in reading a very interesting play or romance, we measure time very inaccurately; and hence, if a play greatly affects our passions, the absurdities of passing over many days or years, and of perpetual changes of place, are not perceived by the audience; as is experienced by every one, who reads or sees some plays of the immortal Shakespear; but it is necessary for inferior authors to observe those rules . . . inculcated by Aristotle, because their works do not interest the passions sufficiently to produce complete reverie.[21]

At one point in the *Biographia Literaria,* Coleridge speaks reluctantly about Darwin's pedantry and highly intellectual use of old categories; and implies, as he does throughout his criticism, that Darwin's careful juggling of distinctions (some of Darwin's jugglings are not careful, but Coleridge objects even to the careful ones) is tedious and foolish compared to the poetic penetration to organic unities. But within a page Coleridge is doing the same thing himself. Just as Darwin in *Zoonomia* and *Phytologia* understood the organic, plantlike connections of all life but made them seem more mechanical by using categorical discourse and analogy, so Coleridge in *Biographia Literaria* explains organic synthesis in literature but continually breaks the synthesis with distinctions and qualifications—with intellectuality. Although *Zoonomia* is a medical treatise and although the *Biographia Literaria* is literary criticism, the two works are very similar in their circular diffuseness, as when Coleridge writes:

> The first lesson of philosophic discipline is to wean the student's attention from the DEGREES of things, which alone form the vocabulary of common life, and to direct it to the KIND abstracted from *degree.* . . . In such discourse the instructor has no other alternative than either to use old words with new meanings (the plan adopted by Darwin in his Zoonomia, or to introduce new terms, after the example of Linnaeus, and the framers of the present chemical nomenculture. The latter mode is evidently preferable, were it only that the former demands a twofold exertion of thought in one and the same act. For the reader, or hearer, is required not only to

learn and bear in mind the new definition; but to unlearn, and keep out of his view, the old and habitual meaning; a far more difficult and perplexing task, and for which the mere *semblance* of eschewing pedantry seems to me an inadequate compensation.[22]

Thus, although Coleridge in particular eschews it, the literary effect that much of his writing creates is that of manifold exertion of thought; and Dr. Darwin is one of his masters.

Even with all this negative influence, however, it should still be pointed out that Darwin helped to lay the intellectual foundation for what Morse Peckham calls "organicism."[23] Even though Darwin himself held back from the acceptance of organicism, his influence on Coleridge and Wordsworth should finally be discussed in terms of organicism. As we have noted, Darwin did not fully believe in organicism; but his poems at the end of the century embodied the most extravagant statements of the principle of a living universe, of the notion of joy permeating all nature, and of personified plant life. Organicism was simply the extension of and full acquiescence to these ideas so that what Meyer Abrams calls "the theory of vegetable genius" could be put into practice. Although, as Abrams indicates, the notion of describing human nature and creativity in terms of plant growth goes well back into the eighteenth century, particularly in German thought, Darwin would certainly be a source of the idea for both Coleridge and Wordsworth.[24]

In a way, this plugging into the paradoxes of a living universe in which one loses his life in order to save it is also a revitalizing of images from the Bible. For example, the first Psalm uses the plant image to describe the spiritually, or imaginatively, alive person:

Blessed is the man that walketh not in the counsel of the ungodly, nor standeth in the way of sinners, nor sitteth in the seat of the scornful . . .

And he shall be like a tree planted by the rivers of water, that bringeth forth his fruit in his season; his leaf also shall not wither; and whatsoever he doeth shall prosper.

The ungodly *are* not so: but *are* like the chaff which the wind driveth away.

It takes a great deal of psychic energy to maintain the belief that some plants do not turn to chaff—that death can be overcome within the natural processes of organic growth. Darwin was ruthlessly tough-minded and "scornful," so that, even though he wrote about the vegetable power in all of us, he never let himself become illusioned that his was an adequate description of human nature. Human nature, for him, was always less like the perfect flower and more like the chaff, the something different, that could not be saved.

III *Shelley*

Shelley, like Darwin, could not accept the plant-growth definition of human nature and human salvation, but neither could he live with Darwin's skeptical, comic materialism for long. Shelley finally forged himself a belief that placed no value on the organic realities of this world (let life triumph); instead, he placed all value on the human will to love and on Neoplatonic otherworldly realities. Strangely enough, Shelley seems quite indebted to Darwin's ideas, especially in his later Neoplatonic beliefs; and the reason is that, even though eventually Shelley renounced all details of this world, he still had to find images and rhetorical devices with which to clothe his Platonism. He used, in general, details derived from his earlier fascination with science and, in particular, glittery, garish imagery reminiscent of *The Botanic Garden*. In other words, the "dome of many-coloured glass" that he was continually trying to break through was colored with glossy images from Darwin's materialism.[25] Indeed, Desmond King-Hele thinks that Shelley, of all the Romantics, benefited the most from Darwin's writings: "when Shelley came to develop his unique style of 'lyricized science,' Darwin's work was the obvious starting point. And, more important, Darwin had been unjustly attacked by reactionaries. . . . Shelley automatically admired anyone who had been vilified because he glowed with too ardent a love for freedom, and this alone is enough to explain his addiction to Darwin."[26]

In his early work, Shelley could benefit directly from Darwin, not only from his atheism and radicalism, but also from his theories and descriptions of nature. For example, Darwin's elaborate attempt in *Zoonomia* to explain all animal events in terms of "catenation of motion" must have supported Shelley in what K. N. Cameron calls his "Necessitarianism."Although Godwin and the French materialists were the greatest influence on Shelley's notion of Necessity, he certainly found supporting detail also in *Zoonomia;* and Cameron, elsewhere in his book, makes the case strongly that Shelley knew Darwin's work well.[27]

Indeed, the notes to "Queen Mab" that describe Necessity read much like Darwin's daring attempts to find links-and-motion relationships between all things from physics to literary criticism. In fact, this encyclopedic expansiveness of Shelley the early pamphleteer and note writer is exactly the effect that all of Darwin's encyclopedic poems and treatises give. Shelley, at first, is an atheist, a materialist, and a necessitarian.

Darwin's notion of the transmission of willed characteristics in evolution, as he explains it in the section "Of Generation" in *Zoonomia* (see Chapter 3 above), is not really a very grand notion of either free will or love. As for the relationship of these concepts of Darwin to the direction that Shelley's later ideas took, he asserted in his last works, the most grandiose hopes for man's freedom of will; and he placed love at the center of man's free existence. Darwin's works about love and sexual pleasure undoubtedly bolstered Shelley's championing of love in "Epipsychidion" and *Prometheus Unbound;* but, when Darwin talked about love, it was mostly with a slightly facetious tone. He talked mostly about sex, and then about comic, married love as a compromise solution to the problem of never achieving total love. Shelley saw no limits to love, and "Epipsychidion" in particular is a breathless celebration of ideal, perfect union. If he learned anything from Darwin's *Zoonomia* about controlling sexuality, he certainly improved on the Doctor's cynicism.

Shelley's greatest improvement, however, was in the versification of scientifically understood phenomena. Shelley literally goes all the way in intellectualizing and humanizing natural events. His later poetry attributes human will to everything in nature, which is going several steps further than comically asserting that there is something human over-against phenomena. Perhaps Shelley did learn from Darwin the basic figure of speech for saying that a thunderstorm, for instance, is an act of love (as he does in "The Cloud" and as Darwin does in several meteorological anecdotes in "The Economy of Vegetation" that were quoted earlier in this book). But in Shelley the implications are taken literally; and the result is a more energetic version of versified science, if perhaps a little more illusioned.

"The Cloud" is often cited as an example of Darwin's influence on Shelley, but the influence may also be seen in *Prometheus Unbound,* a much greater poem.[28] Milton Wilson, in his fine study of the poem, says that the main focus has to be on "the meanwhile" because Shelley has no way of describing what things will be like after the revolution of love.[29] Thus, a characteristic passage in *Prometheus Unbound* will describe and animate phenomena only to say that this will all have to pass, as in the following discussion between two fauns early in the play:

> *I have heard those more skilled in spirits say,*
> *The bubbles, which the enchantment of the sun*
> *Sucks from the pale faint water-flowers that pave*
> *The cozy bottom of clear lakes and pools,*
> *Are the pavilions where such dwell and float*
> *Under the green and golden atmosphere*
> *Which noontide kindles through the woven leaves;*
> *And when these burst, and the thin fiery air,*
> *The which they breathed within those lucent domes,*
> *Ascends to flow like meteors through the night,*
> *They ride on them, and rein headlong speed,*
> *And bow their burning crests, and glide in fire*
> *Under the waters of the earth again.*
>   First Faun. *If such live thus, have others other lives,*
> *Under pink blossoms or within the bells*
> *Of meadow flowers, or folded violets deep,*
> *Or on their dying odours, when they die,*
> *Or in the sunlight of the sphered dew?*
>   Second Faun. *Ay, many more which we may well divine.*
> *But, should we stay to speak, noontide would come,*
> *And thwart Silenus find his goats undrawn,*
> *And grudge to sing those wise and lovely songs*
> *Of Fate, and Chance, and God, and Chaos old,*[30]

Shelley is fascinated by the Darwinian world of amorous elements, water images, and electricity; but he must also develop the abstractions of the poem. His passage seems even more evanescent and vital than Darwin, possibly because he is a better poet or because he believes more fully in the animation of all nature.

Later in Shelley's play, after Prometheus is set free but before Earth gets totally dissolved in the revolution, she speaks; and one of her speeches sounds to me much like Darwin's paean to birth at the end of Canto IV of "The Economy of Vegetation" (quoted in Chapter 2 above). Here again, Shelley states that he is only describing the "meanwhile," and perhaps for that reason the animation of natural phenomena seems even more vital than in Darwin:

> The Earth.   *I hear, I feel;*
> *The lips [Prometheus] are on me, and their touch runs down*
> *Even to the adamantine central gloom*
> *Along these marble nerves; 'tis life, 'tis joy,*
> *And through my withered, old, and icy frame*
> *The warmth of an immortal youth shoots down*
> *Circling. Henceforth the many children fair*
> *Folded in my sustaining arms; all plants,*
> *And creeping forms, and insects rainbow-winged,*
> *And birds, and beasts, and fish, and human shapes,*
> *Which drew disease and pain from my wan bosom,*
> *Draining the poison of despair, shall take*
> *And interchange sweet nutriment; . . .*
> *Death is the veil which those who live call life:*
> *They sleep, and it is lifted: and meanwhile*
> *In mild variety the seasons mild*
> *With rainbow-skirted showers, and oderous winds,*
> *And long blue meteors cleansing the dull night,*
> *And the life-kindling shafts of the keen sun's*
> *All-piercing bow, and the dew-mingled rain*
> *Of the calm moonbeams, a soft influence mild,*
> *Shall clothe the forests and the fields, ay, even*
> *The crag-built deserts of the barren deep,*
> *With ever-living leaves, and fruits, and flowers.* [31]

Darwin wrote of the earth, using his characteristic circular imagery, that "the vast surface kindles as it rolls."[32] Shelley takes this vitalism and kindles it further, right beyond the material world. But, before the revolution actually comes, he writes many lines that seem indebted to Darwin's vibrant descriptions of circling seeds, misty planets, and panting lovers.

IV *Keats*

The well-known difference between Shelley and Keats as craftsmen of Romantic verse can be illustrated by the different kinds of imagery that appealed to them in Darwin.[33] Darwin's images of the misty, evanescent, and amorous forces of electricity and water vapor were what interested Shelley[34], but Keats responded to the more solid images of buds and vases in Darwin. In fact, Keats harks back to the organicism of the early Romantics and to the acceptance of ripeness in material things. Bernard Blackstone, who more than any other critic has discovered profound analogies between Keats and Darwin, observes that, in addition to their being associated with medicine, both used images from animal and plant anatomy in their verse: "There was an attraction, and I think it was primarily an attraction of subject, not of style: Keats liked Darwin's morphology, his buds and fruits and seed-cases (the illustrations are a pleasing feature of *The Botanic Garden*)."[35] Philip Ritterbush has recently expanded Blackstone's ideas to suggest that the pattern of Keats's entire career follows that of Darwin's:

> The literary scholar Bernard Blackstone has drawn a parallel between the urn, the human work of art, and the fruit, swollen by genial growth. This was Keats' "vast idea," as he called it in *Sleep and Poetry* (1818), "The end and aim of Poesy." Also in this poem he wrote of "the small Breath of new buds and unfolding." The swelling of organic forms is a recurrent feature of Keats' poetry, abundantly suggestive of the culminating symbol of the experience of beauty, the Grecian Urn. Blackstone points out that the two volumes of Erasmus Darwin's *Botanic Garden* had opened in 1789 with drawings of cross-sections of flowers and concluded in 1791 with engravings (by William Blake) of the Portland Vase.[36]

I hesitate to insist on such elaborate analogies between the poetry of Darwin and Keats; for, like each of the Romantics, Keats disavowed any influence from Darwin: in a letter of 1816, he thought it "no mean gratification to become acquainted with Men who in their admiration of Poetry do not jumble together Shakespeare and Darwin."[37] But Keats could not have helped being aware of literary devices that Darwin had used flamboyantly and that he himself was attempting to revitalize. In particular, the use of Greek myth was something that Keats took very seriously toward the end of his short career. Indeed, Darwin's poeticizing of the Eleusinian mysteries and his lengthy footnotes are to modern mythographers such as Jacob Bryant and William Warburton, what helped to pave the way for Keats's experiments in a poem like *Hyperion*.[38]

A more important device that, in fact, becomes Keats's major subject matter is the verbal thickness, the rich, sensuous texture involved in capturing the "ripe" moment. Many critics agree Keats finally realized that he could never, as he desired to do, use myth and ideas to discover significant knowledge. In other words, even though he tries ambitiously for ideas, Keats's final literary effect in his greatest poems, such as the odes of 1819 and the ode "To Autumn," is one of skepticism—the same familiar pattern of Darwin's quest for knowledge. Also like Darwin, Keats had to invent some compensation for the absence of knowledge; and Walter Jackson Bate has described beautifully the profound vision that Keats was developing into the dilemma of human aloneness and ignorance:

only a year before [1818], that "eternal fierce destruction" whereby one thing feeds on another, [had he been reading *Zoonomia?*] which shocks the heart when we look "too far into the sea," could seem somewhat more alien to the nature of life and separable from it in our thinking. But the moments were now increasing when much of what we include in the word "evil" seemed inextricably knit into the very nature of that same finitude which also permits a finite creature to exist at all: death, the transitoriness in other ways of what we love, the sheer fact that we cannot proceed in one direction without giving up the opportunity to proceed in others, and that the capacity to enjoy the present moment is as limited and elusive as the present itself. So also with the sharp eager concentration of the living creature as, in its brief finitude, it hurries instinctively to its purposes, enmeshed in activity from the moment of its birth: inevitably its focus is limited and distorted.[39]

The beauty of this dilemma is that the full facing of it, as Keats did, produces a sense of fulfilled joy, the tragic joy of ripeness. As we have noted, Darwin always held back from this tragic joy, just as he held back from the immense self-discovery of Wordsworth and Coleridge: and Darwin's compensation for the absence of knowledge becomes his glittery laughter and nervous rationality. But perhaps his glitter also helped to teach Keats his compensation—how "to load every rift with ore." When we compare the following description of the sexual awakening of butterflies from *The Temple of Nature* to the famous "frozen moment" of Madeline going to sleep from *The Eve of St. Agnes,* which is quoted immediately following, we should note the change from Darwin's facetiousness to Keats's seriousness:

> *Web within web involves his larva form,*
> *Alike secured from sunshine and from storm;*
> *For twelve long days He dreams of blossom'd groves,*
> *Untasted honey, and ideal loves;*
> *Wakes from his trance, alarm'd with young Desire,*
> *Finds his new sex, and feels ecstatic fire.*

. . . .

> *Flown, like a thought, until the morrow-day;*
> *Blissfully havened both from joy and pain;*
> *Clasped like a missal where swart Paynims pray;*
> *Blinded alike from sunshine and from rain,*
> *As though a rose should shut, and be a bud again.*[40]

Aside from Keats's fourth line that seems to be *almost* a literal borrowing of Darwin's second line, the passages are the reverse of each other: the first waking up to bouncy, facetious love, the second heavy with serious fulfillment. In any case, for both Keats and Darwin skepticism forces them to cherish the budding moment of fulfillment. Darwin does so with laughter because he realizes how tenuous such moments are; Keats, who bears down heavily with organic sensuousness, hopes the continual Romantic hope: that he will be able to forge solidity through a concrete rendering of flux and change.

V *Byron*

Whereas each of the other Romantics—Wordsworth, Coleridge, Shelley, Keats—looked for, and succeeded in finding, discoveries in the real world (the objective correlatives) to substantiate their belief in a new human significance, Lord Byron looked only in himself for significance; and he was, therefore, the most skeptical of the Romantics. As a result, the literary effect of his great poem, *Don Juan,* is not one of sensuous imagery or of transcendental insight but one almost entirely of the voice. And the voice, of course, is a laughing, twisting, amorphous voice that finally achieves what we might call "permanence" because of its very variety. In other words, Byron at his mature best is a comic writer who does not believe in free will—or in anything—but who talks about this skepticism enough, and with enough changes in tone, that he creates the only freedom possible: a kind of freedom in despair, a freedom of voice.

Although King-Hele stretches somewhat to find some echoes of Darwin in Byron's thought, there are really no direct echoes.[41] Byron included a verse paragraph on Darwin in his early attack on everyone, but the passage in *English Bards and Scotch Reviewers* does not tell us much more than that Byron was flailing around in search of his own voice. In fact, he calls Darwin: "That mighty master of unmeaning rhyme,/Whose gilded cymbals, more adorn'd than clear,/The eye delighted, but fatigued the ear; . . ."[42] Byron attributes to Darwin exactly what the speaker in *Don Juan* does in years to come: he fatigues with the somewhat unclear variety of his voice.[43] It may seem suspicious to celebrate literature for being unclear; but, if a writer finds that there are no clear ideas to deal with, the one solution open to him is to do a stylistic dance around this absence of knowledge. Without doubt, Lord Byron has taught us much about the complexities of tone and comic dancing, but Darwin too was beginning to take first steps in this modern, skeptical dance.

A recent article on the Gothic novel argues that Byron is closer to the "cosmic despair" (skepticism) of unresolved paradoxes, which the Gothic novel expresses, than he is to the Romantic belief. Although Darwin again is left unnoticed, the following interpretation of Byron could be applied with profit to Darwin: "where Gothic remains darkened by the necessary ambiguities of its conclusions, romantic writing assumes the ultimate existence, if not the easy accessibility, of clear answers to the problems which torment man in this world. . . . a writer like Byron seems closer to the Gothic camp than to the romantics. . . . Perhaps it is his Augustan affinities which so severely undermine his faith in the transcendent power of imagination, but Byron's cosmic despair is not offset even by his glorying in the mysterious grandeur of heroes modeled on himself. . . . Byron shows few signs of faith in the romantic metaphysic; his escape from his existential predicament, if it comes at all, comes in the comic perspective of *Don Juan*."[44]

Thus, even though in Byron there are fewer direct echoes of Darwin, I hear the most meaningful echo of all in a similar literary effect. In fact, to me Byron and Darwin sound the most modern of all the poets discussed in this chapter because they have no illusions whatsoever. And despite the fact that they never met (Byron did meet Dr. Francis Darwin, one of Erasmus Darwin's sons),[45] I think Byron would have liked the honest, old stammering Doctor, who in spite of his stammer, or perhaps because of it, invented a distinctive voice in his writing.

VI *Conclusion*

To be a writer, as Darwin was, writing just before a great revolutionary change in literature proves difficult on one's future literary reputation and evaluation. Darwin could have had little idea, of course, how obsolete his writings would seem in the second half of the twentieth century. His philosophic and scientific ideas seem more contemporary to us, and he is generally given some mention in the histories of science as an early evolutionist. It is in the histories of literature, however, that he needs to be taken more seriously, and here as a writer not an evolutionist, for to continue to have our histories of literature blinded by the glory of the Romantic revolution is to be myopic indeed. Darwin needs to be seen in a new light as a writer.

Although medicine, theoretical natural philosophy (science), and technology occupied much of Darwin's energy, he found time to produce a remarkable amount of highly literary writing. He possessed the familiar traits of the writer: a desire for literary fame coupled with a reticence and lack of self-confidence that forced him to write more and more to prove his genius. He used his scientific interests to provide subject matter for his writings in a way that the twentieth century should find particularly interesting, but most significant was his continual effort to make this scientific material literary. Darwin worked hard at being a writer, even a poet, and this should not be forgotten. He also possessed the writer's fascination with language, with the tricks and texture of language; and he wanted to use these tricks of language to help solve human problems. Darwin is seldom mentioned as a moral writer, one interested in improving man's relation to man; but the meaning of his comic literary effect is literally to help men lead their lives.

Despite these characteristics of the true writer, Darwin will no doubt always be categorized as a minor writer: never quite doing what he intended to do with enough force. But most writers are minor writers in this sense, and they seem more human to us for it. Perhaps the final word on Darwin here should come from a scientist, since Darwin's skepticism was the Lockean skepticism of the scientist. The following tribute by Loren Eiseley is not actually to Erasmus Darwin, but to his continuing seed and grandson, Charles Darwin. It is significant and ironic that Darwin's own individuality, which his comic defense maintained, is not finally what will be described in this book about him. Or, in another sense, this simply proves the Doctor right: he has lost his individuality, but his "catenation" with a grandson that he never saw carries on. The following statement speaks for them both, except that the older Darwin laughed a lot in his pity:

None of his forerunners has left us such a message; none saw, in a similar manner, the whole vista of life with quite such sweeping vision. None, it may be added, spoke with the pity which infuses these lines: "If we choose to let conjecture run wild, then animals, our fellow brethren in pain, disease, suffering and famine—our slaves in the most laborious works, our companions in our amusements—they may partake of our origin in one common ancestor—we may be all melted together."[46]

Notes and References

Preface

1. For the most complete history of the Lunar Society see Robert E. Schofield, *The Lunar Society of Birmingham* (Oxford, 1963).

2. *The Essential Writings of Erasmus Darwin,* chosen and edited with a linking commentary by Desmond King-Hele (London, 1968).

Chapter One

1. Peter Gay, *The Enlightenment: An Interpretation* (New York, 1965). For an explanation of the international occurrence of the *philosophe,* see pp. 10 f.

2. Philip C. Ritterbush, *Overtures to Biology, The Speculations of Eighteenth-Century Naturalists* (New Haven and London, 1964), p. viii.

3. Although Haller was a staunch Deist and Darwin, I believe, finally was not, there are other interesting similarities between the two men. Both were eminent doctors; both wrote couplet-type verse on science; but Haller refused to speculate as much as Darwin, and so remained a Deist. The dedication, then, from La Mettrie, the atheist, to Haller was probably meant ironically. See Howard Mumford Jones, "Albrecht von Haller and English Philosophy," in *Publications of the Modern Language Association,* XL (1925), 103–27.

4. Schofield, p. 26. Quoted from John Alfred Langford, *A Century of Birmingham Life* (Birmingham, 1868), 148.

5. Erasmus Darwin, *Zoonomia; or, The Laws of Organic Life* (London, 1794–96), I, 455.

6. See Ritterbush, p. 167.

7. David Hartley, *Observations on Man* (1749) in Leonard M. Trawick, ed., *Backgrounds of Romanticism* (Bloomington and London, 1967), p. 71.

8. *The Temple of Nature* (London, 1803), p. 95, note to Canto III, l. 144.

9. See especially Chapter 1 in Ernest Lee Tuveson, *The Imagination as a Means of Grace, Locke and the Aesthetics of Romanticism* (Berkeley and Los Angeles, 1960).

10. *Temple,* p. 99 of "Additional Notes," Note XIV.

11. *Zoonomia,* I, 64.

12. Letter to Robert Waring Darwin, quoted by Charles Darwin,

114

"Preliminary Notice" to Ernst Krause, *Erasmus Darwin* (London, 1879), pp. 49–50.

13. *Zoonomia,* I, 4.

14. For a good general introduction to the materialistic monism of the pre-Socratics, Epicurus, and Lucretius see Russel M. Geer's introduction to his translation of Lucretius, *On Nature* (New York, 1965). Darwin quotes from Lucretius frequently, and one of his most eloquent notes reminds me of Heraclitus; see below, Note 19.

15. *Temple,* Additional notes I and VIII, pp. 1, 38.

16. See Bentley Glass, Owsei Temkin, and William L. Straus, Jr., eds., *Forerunners of Darwin 1745–1859* (Baltimore, 1959). Especially see the articles by Francis C. Haber and Charles Coulston Gillispie.

17. *Zoonomia,* I, 505, 509. Note that by the time he wrote the note to *The Temple of Nature* quoted above his speculation had progressed to where he was suggesting that all life, vegetable and all animal (not just warm-blooded), developed from an original "filament."

18. See Geer's introduction to Lucretius above.

19. Darwin, *Temple,* note to Canto IV, l. 453, 166–67.

20. See Ralph B. Crum, *Scientific Thought in Poetry* (New York, 1931), pp. 118–19.

21. Erasmus Darwin, "Remarks on the Opinion of Henry Eeles, Esq., Concerning the Ascent of Vapour" in *Philosophical Transactions of the Royal Society,* L (1757), 248–49.

22. See "Ode: Intimations of Immortality," l. 149.

23. Godwin, for example, places more emphasis on improvement than Darwin does, but in both there is a dizzying sense of flux: "The term perfectible, thus explained, not only does not imply the capacity of being brought to perfection but stands in express opposition to it. If we could arrive at perfection, there would be an end to our improvement." From William Godwin, *Enquiry Concerning Political Justice . . . .* in Trawick, p. 202. Lois Whitney's comments on Darwin conclude that, even though he wrote often of perfectibility, his vision was primarily one of fascination with random change. Lois Whitney, *Primitivism and the Idea of Progress* (New York, 1965), p. 159. Originally published 1934.

24. See Bertrand Russell's introduction to Frederick Albert Lange, *The History of Materialism* (New York, 1950), p. xi. (originally published 1865).

25. I am using Carl Becker's apt borrowing from Aristophanes. See Carl L. Becker, *The Heavenly City of the Eighteenth-Century Philosophers* (New Haven, 1932), p. 15.

26. For La Mettrie and Diderot, see the fine introductions by Otis E. Fellows and Norman L. Torrey in their anthology, *The Age of Enlightenment* (New York, 1942). For Hume, see the chapter on him in Peter Gay, *The Enlightenment* (New York, 1966).

27. A notorious example is the pious Albrecht von Haller who refused to

see the humor in La Mettrie's dedication of *L'Homme Machine* to him. In a published letter of disavowal, Haller wrote morosely: "I regard its dedication to myself as an outrage, exceeding in cruelty all those which its anonymous author has inflicted on so many worthy people, and I beg the members of the public to be assured that I have never had anything to do with the author of *L'Homme Machine,* that I do not know him, that he is in no way a friend of mine, and that I should look upon any consonance of views between us as one of the most unmitigated calamities that could possibly befall me." Quoted in Paul Hazard, *European Thought in the Eighteenth Century* (New Haven, 1954), p. 128. Also, see Note 3 above.

28. Hesketh Pearson, *Doctor Darwin* (New York, 1963). Originally published 1930.

29. See *Zoonomia,* I, 518–19.

30. *Ibid.,* p. 391.

31. See Frank Manuel, *The Eighteenth Century Confronts the Gods* (Cambridge, Mass., 1959), p. 65.

32. William Warburton's *Divine Legation of Moses* (London, 1738–41) was followed by other double-truth interpretations of ancient myth, notably Jacob Bryant's *A New System; or, An Analysis of Antient Mythology* (London, 1774–76). Darwin used and referred to both books.

33. Irwin Primer, "Erasmus Darwin's *Temple of Nature:* Progress, Evolution, and the Eleusinian Mysteries," *Journal of the History of Ideas,* XXV (January-March, 1964), 65–66.

34. *Ibid.,* pp. 68–75. The parody of Darwin's verse in the *Anti-Jacobin* certainly hurt his literary reputation. See Norton Garfinkle, "Science and Religion in England, 1790–1800: The Critical Response to the Work of Erasmus Darwin," *Journal of the History of Ideas,* XVI (June, 1955), 376–88.

35. Geoffrey H. Hartman, *Wordsworth's Poetry 1787–1814* (New Haven and London, 1964), p. 391. Hartman's book also contains an apt expression of the assumption behind my reading of Darwin: "[Eighteenth-century science was] . . . visionary thought masking as natural philosophy." *Ibid.,* p. 196.

36. Elizabeth Sewell, *The Orphic Voice* (New Haven and London, 1960), p. 209. She very ambitiously puts Darwin into what she calls the Orphic tradition along with Wordsworth, Goethe, and others.

37. Although I had noticed the theme of circularity in Darwin and begun working with it before I read Poulet's book on the circle, I am immensely indebted to his provocative discussion. See Georges Poulet, *The Metamorphoses of the Circle,* Carley Dawson and Elliot Coleman, trans. (Baltimore, 1966).

38. *The Temple of Nature* (London, 1803), Canto III, 11. 385–88.

39. Anna Seward, *Memoirs of the Life of Dr. Darwin* (London, 1804), pp. 2–4, 77.

40. Elizabeth Schneider, *Coleridge, Opium and Kubla Khan* (Chicago, 1953), pp. 106–9.

41. Oliver Elton, *A Survey of English Literature 1780–1880* (New York, 1913), I, 44.

42. In a study of Thomas Lovell Beddoes, the admiration of Dr. Beddoes, the poet's father, for Darwin is made clear: "The immediate stimulus to Dr. Beddoes' poem was given by the assertion of some of his friends that the style of Dr. Darwin was impossible to imitate. Dr. Beddoes' admiration for Darwin was great, and his familiarity with his poetical style made his imitation so successful that he was able to pass off portions of his work as Darwin's when reading it to these very men." H. W. Donner, *Thomas Lovell Beddoes* (Oxford, 1935), p. 39.

43. *Ibid.,* p. 38. Beddoes, of course, only produced one twelfth the amount of verse as Darwin.

44. Robert Scholes, *The Fabulators* (New York, 1967), p. 171.

45. From "Apology," "The Economy of Vegetation," Part I, *The Botanic Garden* (London, 1791), p. vii.

46. *The Temple of Nature,* note to Canto II, 1.47, p. 47. The most common sources for Darwin's notions about the mythological stories which he uses in his text are, in addition to Warburton and Bryant, mentioned above: Sir Francis Bacon, *De Sapientia Veterum* (1609); *The Wisedome of the Ancients* (1619). Joseph Spence, *Polymetis: or, An Enquiry Concerning the Agreement Between the Works of the Roman Poets, and the Remains of the Antient Artists* (1747). Pierre Danet, *A Complete Dictionary of the Greek and Roman Antiquities* (1700). Irwin Primer writes about Darwin's use of myth: "Darwin's footnotes show that his interpretation of the myths was at times in the tradition of physical allegorism (myth as allegory or dim intuition of the operations of Nature), and at times in the tradition of the Euhemerists who regarded the gods as former heroes and great men deified. In any event, his interest in mythology derives not only from the literary heritage of antiquity but also (and perhaps more directly) from theologians and historians of human culture in his own century." Primer, p. 66.

47. From "Proem," "The Loves of the Plants," Part II, *The Botanic Garden* (London, 1789), p. xv.

48. For a much more detailed discussion of Darwin's rhetoric, diction, and prosody see my unpublished dissertation "The Poems of Erasmus Darwin" (Columbia Univ., 1967).

49. William K. Wimsatt, Jr., introduction to *Selected Poetry and Prose of Alexander Pope* (New York, 1951), p. xxv.

50. Charles Darwin, preliminary notice to Ernst Krause, *Erasmus Darwin* (London, 1879), p. 10.

51. Primer, p. 62.

52. Poulet, p. xvi. The word "schiastic" in the quotation is either an error in the Baltimore text or a variant spelling of chiastic.

53. "The Loves of the Plants," Canto I, 11. 51–52.

54. *Ibid.,* Canto I, 11. 167–68.

55. "The Economy of Vegetation," Canto II, 11. 81–82.

56. *Ibid.,* Canto II, 11. 523–24.

57. *Ibid.,* Canto III, 11. 465–68.

58. "The Loves of the Plants," Canto II, 11. 115–38.

59. "The Economy of Vegetation," Canto III, 11. 185–86.

60. *Ibid.,* Canto III, 11. 197–98.

61. *Ibid.,* Canto III, 11. 391–92.

62. *The Temple of Nature,* Canto I, 11. 333–34.

63. *Ibid.,* Canto II, 11. 41–42.

64. Seward, p. 177.

65. This periphrasis is from James Thomson's *Winter,* 1. 87. In the best study of this matter, John Arthos lists many more. John Arthos, *The Language of Natural Description in 18th-century Poetry* (Ann Arbor, 1949).

66. *The Temple of Nature,* Canto II, 11. 371–76.

67. C. V. Deane, *Aspects of Eighteenth Century Nature Poetry* (Oxford, 1935), p. 46.

68. Austin Warren describes Pope's playful treatment of dangerous topics well. He writes: "*The Rape [of the Lock]* owes its richness and resonance to its overstructure of powerful, dangerous motifs. What keeps it from being that filigree artifice which the romantics saw (and praised) is its playing with fire, especially the fires of sex and religion." Austin Warren, *Rage for Order* (Chicago, 1948), pp. 46–47.

69. *The Temple of Nature,* Canto II, 11. 269–70.

70. See Arthos, p. 361 for the periphrastic diction for birds.

71. W. K. Wimsatt quotes the couplet (pejoratively) without identifying it, and Deane says it is "circumlocution in excelsis from Erasmus Darwin's Botanic Garden." W. K. Wimsatt, Jr., *The Verbal Icon* (New York, 1965), p. 143. Deane, p. 5. I cannot find the couplet either in "The Economy of Vegetation" or in "The Loves of the Plants," but it certainly is consistent with Darwin's style.

72. Darwin cites Buffon often, but the more radical *philosophes,* notably La Mettrie, do not appear in his notes. Nevertheless, Darwin's ideas and tone are much closer to the radical *philosophes,* as Primer's article points out. My argument has elaborated more on the tonal effects related to these radical ideas. See above.

73. Georges-Louis Leclerc, comte de Buffon, *Discours sur le style* (1753) in Fellows and Torrey, p. 601.

Chapter Two

1. Anna Seward, *Memoirs of the Life of Dr. Darwin* (London, 1804), pp. 3–4.

2. *Ibid.,* pp. 125–32 and p. 167.

3. Hesketh Pearson, in his biography of Darwin, gives a rather weak explanation that makes Darwin seem less dishonest in this plagiarism. First, he quotes a flippant remark of Darwin's to the effect that he was intending to compliment Miss Seward, but Darwin gives no acknowledgment in his book to Miss Seward. Then Pearson speculated that Darwin was doing her the favor of not attributing lines to her that he himself had changed. Hesketh Pearson, *Doctor Darwin* (New York, 1963), p. 208. My judgment is that the borrowing is simply plagiarism, which Darwin himself describes well in a prose interlude to "The Loves of the Plants": "It may be difficult to mark the exact boundary of what should be termed plagiarism: where the sentiment and expression are both borrowed without due acknowledgement, there can be no doubt;—single words, on the contrary, taken from other authors, cannot convict a writer of plagiarism: they are lawful game, wild by nature, the property of all who can capture them ...." Erasmus Darwin, *The Botanic Garden, Part II* (London, 1799), fifth edition, pp. 184–85.

4. See Albert S. Roe, "The Thunder of Egypt—Blake and Erasmus Darwin," in Alvin H. Rosenfeld, ed., *William Blake Essays for S. Foster Damon* (Providence, 1969), pp. 159–69.

5. Seward, *Memoirs* .... She had not seen *The Temple of Nature,* but devotes nearly 190 pages to paraphrasing *The Botanic Garden.* Both James V. Logan and Desmond King-Hele content themselves with very general summaries of the contents of the poems. Logan, *The Poetry and Aesthetics of Erasmus Darwin* (Princeton, 1936). King-Hele, *Erasmus Darwin* (London, 1963). Leopold Brandl's monographs in German on Darwin's poems are actually mostly plot summary, but he seems to be primarily interested in the scientific content of the plots rather than in their artistic structure. Brandl, *Erasmus Darwin's [sic] Temple of Nature,* (Wien und Leipzig, 1902). Brandl, *Erasmus Darwins Botanic Garden* (Wien und Leipzig, 1909).

6. This first part of the canto is the section that Darwin plagiarized, with a few changes, from Anna Seward. See above.

7. We might speculate on the appropriateness of this definition to all the arts since each seems to try to come to terms with the chaos of experience in order to make something less chaotic out of it. The definition seems particularly appropriate to Darwin's literary strategy and to his comic tone.

8. Photosynthesis was discovered by a Dutch biologist, Jan Ingenhousz. Some of his findings were published in 1779, but a more complete exposition of the process was given in 1796. In any case, Darwin does not mention Ingenhousz. See A. Wolf, *A History of Science, Technology, and Philosophy in the Eighteenth Century,* revised edition (New York, 1952), p. 450.

9. Seward, p. 211.

10. *Ibid.,* p. 285.

11. Irwin Primer, "Erasmus Darwin's *Temple of Nature:* Progress,

Evolution, and Eleusinian Mysteries," in *Journal of the History of Ideas,* XXV (January-March, 1964), 65.

12. The phrase "scenical representations," which is typical of Darwin's emphasis on visual imagery, comes from the explanation in *The Temple of Nature* of the Eleusinian mysteries. *The Temple of Nature* (London, 1803), Canto I, note to 1. 137, p. 13.

13. Additional notes to *The Botanic Garden, Part I* (London, 1791), p. 54.

14. *Ibid.,* pp. 55–57.

15. *Ibid.,* p. 58.

16. A recent book on the Eleusinian mysteries makes it clear that Darwin and his eighteenth-century authorities were mistaken: "In modern times, P. Foucart, noticing the similarities existing between the Eleusinian myth and the Egyptian story of Isis and Osiris and recalling the story of Danaos and his daughters, taught that the Mysteries were introduced to Eleusis from Egypt in the XVIII Dynasty. The great popularity this theory enjoyed for almost a quarter of a century has declined considerably. In 1927, Charles Picard proved that the theory was untenable and pointed out that not a single object of Egyptian origin, or indicating Egyptian influence, and dating from the second millennium was found in the Sanctuary of Eleusis." George E. Mylonas, *Eleusis and the Eleusinian Mysteries* (Princeton, 1961), p. 15.

17. *The Botanic Garden, Part I,* pp. vii-viii.

18. *The Temple of Nature,* Canto I, note to 1. 137, p. 13.

19. Additional notes to *The Botanic Garden, Part I,* p. 54.

20. Seward, p. 169.

21. Primer calls this the "myth of the eternal return" and gives a fine description of it. He also credits Elizabeth Sewell with being the first to point it out in Darwin. Primer, pp. 62–64. See Elizabeth Sewell, *The Orphic Voice* (New Haven, 1960).

22. Sewell, p. 234. It would be interesting here to compare the structure of Byron's *Don Juan,* and even that of Wordworth's *The Prelude,* although such a comparison is beyond the scope of this study.

23. Selections from the poems and prose were published in book form in 1968, but a complete edition is still lacking. See Desmond King-Hele, *The Essential Writings of Erasmus Darwin* (London, 1968).

24. Darwin's parodists in "The Loves of the Triangles" sense this thematic relationship and express it succinctly in Darwin's own facetious tone:

> *For* you, *no Tangents touch, no Angles meet,*
> *No Circles join in osculation sweet!*

note Verse 10 . . .

Ditto, *Osculation*—For the *Osculation,* or kissing of Circles and other Curves, see Huygens, who has veiled this delicate and inflammatory subject in the decent obscurity of a learned language."

Anon., *Poems of the Anti-Jacobin* (London, 1801), p. 125.

25. *The Botanic Garden, Part II,* "Proem," p. XV.

26. Seward, p. 300.

27. See Chapter 1 above for the quotation of this passage in the discussion of word devices such as chiasmus.

28. *The Botanic Garden, Part II,* Canto IV, 11. 465–508.

29. *Ibid.,* p. 236.

30. For a recent provocative summary of the twentieth-century interest in the four elements, see Paul Ginestier, *The Poet and the Machine,* Martin B. Friedman, trans. (Chapel Hill, 1961), p. 14.

31. His commendation was very high indeed: "the twelve verses that by miracle describe and comprehend the creation of the universe out of chaos, are in my opinion the most sublime passage in any author . . . . " Horace Walpole, *The Letters of . . . ,* Mrs. Paget Toynbee, ed. (Oxford, 1905), XV, 110. To Thomas Barrett, May 14, 1792.

32. *The Botanic Garden, Part I,* Canto I, 11. 97–114. The German scholar, Leopold Brandl, who appreciated Darwin's poems to a great extent for their scientific vitality, also admired this passage a great deal. See Brandl, *Erasmus Darwins Botanic Garden* (Wien und Leipzig, 1909), pp. 38–39.

33. Darwin may have gotten his notion of hermaphroditism in the gods and goddesses of myth from Jacob Bryant where the following interesting discussion appears: "But the most extraordinary circumstance was, that they represented the same Deity of different sexes. A bearded Apollo was uncommon; but Venus with a beard must have been very extraordinary. Yet she is said to have been thus exhibited in Cyprus, under the name of Aphroditus, . . . The poet Calvus speaks of her as masculine: *Polientemque Deum Venerem.* Valerius Soranus among other titles calls Jupiter the mother of the Gods." Jacob Bryant, *A New System; or, an Analysis of Antient Mythology* (London, 1807), I, 392.

34. *The Botanic Garden, Part I,* p. 8.

35. *Ibid.,* Canto II, 11. 59–66, p. 63.

36. *Ibid.,* Canto II, 11. 151–82.

37. *Ibid.,* pp. 81–82.

38. *Ibid.,* Canto III, 11. 201–60, pp. 136–37.

39. *Ibid.,* Canto IV, 11. 29–48, 59–62.

40. Professor Howard Vincent of Kent State University made this observation about Williams' poetry in a symposium at Kent in February, 1966.

41. *The Botanic Garden, Part I,* Canto IV, 11. 351–408.

42. The egg of night and the idea of metamorphosis suggest the myth of Proteus and his "curved shell." Earl Wasserman says that this myth, and even the notion of circularity, is one of the most successful ideas in Shelley's *Prometheus Unbound.* In fact, Shelley's themes appear very similar to Darwin's as Wasserman describes them. He writes: "[at the end of the play] . . .

the gift of potentiality honoring the union of the One Mind and Love has been exhaled into the actuality of human time as an embracing and world-determining atmosphere of love, corresponding to all the many other symbolic sphere-enclosing atmospheres of the poem." Earl R. Wasserman, Shelley's *Prometheus Unbound, a Critical Reading* (Baltimore, 1965), pp. 178–81. Quotation is from p. 181.

Chapter Three

1. "the central dilemma [by 1870] was the uses of mathematics and the uses of prose. [J. C.] Maxwell [a physicist] inevitably and rightly had to employ the sharper and more nearly accurate instrument of mathematical expression, and so do we." Howard Mumford Jones and I. Bernard Cohen, eds., *Science Before Darwin* (London, 1963), p. 10. W. P. Jones describes something similar and applies it to Darwin's poetry in his chapter entitled "The Didactic Dilemma in Scientific Poetry" in *The Rhetoric of Science* (Berkeley and Los Angeles, 1966), pp. 200 ff.

2. Stanley Edgar Hyman, *The Tangled Bank, Darwin, Marx, Frazer and Freud as Imaginative Writers* (New York, 1962), p. 447.

3. Jones and Cohen, pp. 5–6.

4. Hyman, p. 41.

5. Erasmus Darwin, *Zoonomia,* I (London, 1794), p. 1.

6. *Ibid.,* p. 15.

7. *Ibid.,* p. 19.

8. The clearest definitions of these terms appear on p. 131 of vol. I. of *Zoonomia.*

9. *Zoonomia,* I, 23.

10. *Ibid.,* p. 109. Although Philip C. Ritterbush interprets Darwin's discussion of animal motion more completely as an expression of the spirit-matter dualism, he does hint at what I call Darwin's comic attitude toward the absurdity of such a dualism: "In the poems the cause of life and organic evolution appears to be a faculty of 'love,' which he compared to Newtonian attraction on the purely physical level in nature. This analogy, even if a popular one in Darwin's sense, makes it impossible for us to be sure to what extent he meant to distinguish organic from inorganic energies." Philip C. Ritterbush, *Overtures to Biology* (New Haven and London, 1964), p. 170.

11. *Zoonomia,* I, 133–34.

12. *Ibid.,* p. 503.

13. *Ibid.,* p. 524.

14. *Ibid.,* p. 505 and 509. For Darwin's kinship to the *philosophes,* including David Hume, see Chapter 1. This prose quotation also appears there, but it is good enough to quote again.

15. *Ibid.,* p. 467.

16. *Ibid.,* p. 480.

17. For Anna Seward's description of his stammer and for my earlier consideration of its relation to his comic tone see Chapter 1, Section II, "Double Truth and the Comic Vision."

18. *Zoonomia,* I, 193.

19. Philip C. Ritterbush, *The Art of Organic Forms* (Washington, 1968), pp. 18–19.

20. David Hartley, *Observations on Man* (London, 1749), I, 294.

21. *Zoonomia,* I, 106–7.

22. *Phytologia* (Dublin, 1800), p. vii.

23. *Ibid.,* p. 8. Italics his. If I tried to ascertain the current scientific validity of all Darwin's speculations this book would never be finished, but I came across a newspaper report, while writing this chapter, of recent scientific interest in the possibility of plant consciousness. See the *Cleveland Plain Dealer* for March 14, 1969, p. 1. The headline of the article is "Do Plants Feel Emotional Stresses?"

24. Darwin, *Phytologia,* p. 85.

25. *Ibid.,* p. 92.

26. *Ibid.,* p. 92.

27. *Ibid.,* p. 93.

28. *Ibid.,* p. 125.

29. Earl Wasserman explains this argument very well, concluding that for the Romantics analogy was dead: "which is to say that analogy, being itself meaningless, can no longer organize reality and experience." Earl R. Wasserman, *The Subtler Language* (Baltimore, 1959), p. 182.

30. *Phytologia,* p. 508.

31. *Ibid.,* p. 507.

32. *Ibid.,* p. 508.

33. *Ibid.,* pp. 480–81, 509–11.

34. See Philip C. Ritterbush, "Erasmus Darwin's Second Published Poem," *Review of English Studies,* XIII (1962), 158–60. This is the poem dealing with shorthand.

35. For an account of the technical details in Darwin's theory and practice of metrics, see the chapter on metrics in my unpublished dissertation, "The Poems of Erasmus Darwin" (Columbia Univ., 1967).

36. See the preface in the 1968 facsimile reprint of the book by Johnson Reprint Corporation: Erasmus Darwin, *A Plan for the Conduct of Female Education in Boarding Schools,* with a new Preface (New York, 1968). Originally published 1797.

37. *Ibid.,* pp. 37–38.

38. *Ibid.,* p. 19.

39. *Ibid.,* pp. 55–56.

40. Darwin, *Zoonomia,* I, 148.

41. Darwin, *Phytologia,* p. 295.

42. I am indebted to Judson Jerome for drawing my attention to this distinction in his fine, new poetry textbook, *Poetry: Premeditated Art* (Boston, 1968), pp. 1–3.

43. *The Temple of Nature* (London, 1803), "Additional Notes," p. 38.

Chapter Four

1. *Zoonomia* (London, 1794), I, title page. Dryden's translation of the same lines by comparison seems more abstract and less Falstaffian:

> *Know first, that heaven and earth's compacted frame,*
> *And flowing waters, and the starry flame,*
> *And both the radiant lights, one common soul*
> *Inspires and feeds, and animates the whole.*
> *This active mind infus'd through all the space,*
> *Unites and mingles with the mighty mass.*

John Dryden, translation of the *Aeneid*, Book VI, ll. 980–85.

2. Robert E. Schofield, *The Lunar Society of Birmingham* (Oxford, 1963), p. 402.

3. See the end of Chapter 1 for a discussion of poetic diction in all of Darwin's verse as well as of other devices for "thickening" the sensuous quality of the verse.

4. *The Temple of Nature* (London, 1803), Canto I, ll. 131–32. Irwin Primer relates Darwin's Goddess to other polybreasted female figures that were allegories for nature in eighteenth-century European literature, and especially in illustrations. Irwin Primer, "Erasmus Darwin's *Temple of Nature*: Progress, Evolution, and Eleusinian Mysteries," in *Journal of the History of Ideas*, XXV (January-March, 1964), 58–76.

5. Darwin, *The Temple . . .* , Canto I, ll. 209-14.

6. *Ibid.*, Canto I, ll. 19–20.

7. *Ibid.*, Canto II, ll. 147–58. Later in this poem there is a line that may have suggested to Keats line 242 in *The Eve of St. Agnes* ("Blinded alike from sunshine and from rain"), another skillful creation of sensuousness by Darwin: "Web within web involves his larva form/ Alike secured from sunshine and from storm." Canto II, ll.299–300.

8. *Ibid.*, Canto II, ll. 263–78. Note that one of his devices for achieving the comic tone is the overblown use of poetic diction as in l. 269. I describe in general this use of poetic diction at the end of Chapter 1. Also, notice how the second verse paragraph of this sounds like Wallace Stevens' poem "High-Toned Old Christian Woman."

9. Darwin, *Temple*, Canto IV, l. 526.

10. At the end of Canto I, Darwin writes: "Then hand in hand along the waving glades/ The virgin Sisters pass . . . . " *Ibid.*, Canto I, ll. 421–22.

11. *Ibid.*, Canto IV, l.456.

12. See Chapter 2.

13. See Primer, "Erasmus Darwin's *Temple* . . . . " He corrects Lois Whitney's oversimplification of Darwin's position on progress in her *Primitivism and the Idea of Progress in English Popular Literature of the Eighteenth Century* (New York, 1965).

14. Darwin, *Temple,* note to 1. 122, Canto II, pp. 53–54.

15. *Ibid.,* Canto IV, 11. 123–30.

16. See Hesketh Pearson's account of Darwin's reaction to this tragedy in his life in *Doctor Darwin* (New York, 1963), pp. 220–21.

17. Darwin, *Temple,* Canto IV, 11. 17–28 and 11. 383–402.

18. *Ibid.,* Canto I, 11. 65–74 and 11. 89–96.

19. *Ibid.,* Canto I, 11. 1–3 and 11. 15–32.

20. Note to 1. 207, Canto III, pp. 100–101.

21. Darwin, *Temple,* Canto III, 11. 123–30.

22. *Ibid.,* Canto I, 11. 233–48.

23. *The Orphic Voice* (New Haven, 1960), p. 245.

24. Darwin, *Temple,* Canto IV, 11. 447–62.

Chapter Five

1. See King-Hele, *Erasmus Darwin* (London, 1963), pp. 133–52. A recent article has discovered a possible indebtedness to Darwin in William Cowper's "Yardley Oak," in *English Language Notes,* V, 1 (September, 1967), 27–32. I refer the reader to these explorations of line and word resemblances, but my present chapter attempts to pin down Darwin's larger relationship to the Romantics—in some cases, this involves comparison of lines.

2. Anon., *The Golden Age* (Rivington, London, 1794). See King-Hele's description of it.

3. "The Loves of the Triangles"—"A Mathematical and Philosophical Poem, inscribed to Dr. Darwin" began to appear in installments in *The Anti-Jacobin* on April 16, 1798. Three weeks later, on May 7, the last installment of the parody appeared; it was apparently devastating in its effect on Darwin's literary reputation. The authors of the parody were probably George Canning, Hookham Frere, and George Ellis. Anon., *Poems of the Anti-Jacobin* (London, 1801), pp. 118–51.

4. Thomas Brown, *Observations on the Zoonomia of Erasmus Darwin* (Edinburgh, 1798). For details about the vicious attacks in the 1790's on Darwin's radicalism see Irwin Primer, "Erasmus Darwin's *Temple of Nature:* Progress, Evolution, and Eleusinian Mysteries," in *Journal of Ideas,* XXV (January-March, 1964), 73–74.

5. See Robert L. Chamberlain, "George Crabbe and Darwin's Amorous Plants," *Journal of English and Germanic Philology,* LXI (1962), 852.

6. Mary Anne Schimmelpenninck, *Life of* . . . . (London, 1858), I, 205.

7. Wordsworth, *The Prelude,* Book XIV, 11. 66–74, 113–18.

8. See Wordsworth, "Lines Composed a Few Miles above Tintern Abbey," 1. 49.

9. See Geoffrey H. Hartman, *Wordsworth's Poetry 1787–1814* (New Haven and London), p. 16. Also see *The Prelude,* Book VI, 1. 600.

10. Northrop Frye, *A Study of English Romanticism* (New York, 1968), p. 85.

11. Wordsworth, *The Prelude,* Book XI, 11. 321–23.

12. *Zoonomia,* I, 480. I quoted this passage earlier in the chapter on his scientific writing, and other pages of that chapter are relevant to this discussion. For Wordsworth's acquaintance with *Zoonomia,*see Mark L. Reed, *Wordsworth; the Chronology of the Early Years, 1770–1799* (Cambridge, 1967), p. 224.

13. Wordsworth, "Ode: Intimations of Immortality from Recollections of Early Childhood," 11. 161–67.

14. See Chester F. Chapin, *Personification in Eighteenth-Century English Poetry* (New York, 1968), originally printed 1954, p. 82. Chapin quotes Frederick Pottle as saying, "Wordsworth's famous essay on poetic diction is from beginning to end an anxious attack on the poetry of Erasmus Darwin."

15. Samuel H. Monk, "Anna Seward and the Romantic Poets," in E. L. Griggs, ed., *Wordsworth and Coleridge: Studies in Honor of George McLean Harper* (Princeton, 1939), pp. 124, 133.

16. Samuel Taylor Coleridge, *Shakespearean Criticism,* Thomas Middleton Raysor, ed. (New York, 1960), II, 42. Also see George McLean Harper, "Coleridge's Conversation Poems," in M. H. Abrams, ed., *English Romantic Poets Modern Essays in Criticism* (New York, 1960), p. 147. Harper points out that Coleridge, like Wordsworth, used the devices of "Gaudyverse" in his early career. This debt is not, however, the important debt to Darwin.

17. See in particular John Livingston Lowes, *The Road to Xanadu* (New York, 1959), pp. 32 ff.

18. See Donald M. Hassler, "Coleridge, Darwin, and the Dome," in *The Serif,* IV (September, 1967, 28–31.

19. See earlier in this book as well as Donald M. Hassler, "Erasmus Darwin's Comic Bathos," in *The Serif,* VI, (June, 1969).

20. Elizabeth Schneider, *Coleridge, Opium, and Kubla Khan* (Chicago, 1953), p. 101. For Coleridge's version see Chapter XIV of *Biographia Literaria* and his *Shakespearean Criticism.*

21. Darwin, *Zoonomia,* I, 206–7.

22. Samuel Taylor Coleridge, *Biographia Literaria,* ed. J. Shawcross (Oxford, 1907), I, 108. See the next page (p. 109) for Coleridge's lapse into this very practice.

23. Peckham's article is the best definition and explanation of this

variety of Romanticism. See Morse Peckham, "Toward a Theory of Romanticism," in *Publications of the Modern Language Association,* LXVI (1951), 5–23.

24. See M. H. Abrams, *The Mirror and the Lamp* (New York, 1958), first published 1953, pp. 198–213.

25. Shelley, *Adonais,* 1. 462. Blake, who was much like Shelley in his visionary thought, did not use science as a rhetorical foundation for his Platonism; he used, among other things, a stricter biblical tradition. Thus, Blake had no reason to be indebted to Darwin and, in fact, deliberately stayed away from Darwin more than did any other Romantic. Perhaps this avoidance is partly due to the fact that Blake was hired by Joseph Johnson, Darwin's publisher, to provide some of the illustrations for Darwin's very fashionable poems when Blake himself was an unknown writer.

26. King-Hele, p. 151.

27. See Kenneth Neill Cameron, *The Young Shelley, Genesis of a Radical* (New York, 1962), first published 1950, pp. 281–84. The pioneering study of Shelley's indebtedness to Darwin, however, is Carl H. Grabo, *A Newton Among Poets: Shelley's Use of Science in Prometheus Unbound* (Chapel Hill, 1930). In my judgment, Grabo attributes too much emphasis on free will to Darwin; but his book does establish Shelley's familiarity with Darwin.

28. King-Hele writes on p. 148: "In the *Cloud* the Darwinian flavour is much stronger. Canto III of "The Economy of Vegetation" is largely concerned with clouds and water, and the shower scene (lines 509–36) seems like a preview of [it]."

29. Milton Wilson, *Shelley's Later Poetry: A Study of His Prophetic Imagination* (New York, 1959).

30. *Prometheus Unbound,* Act II, scene II, 11. 70–92.

31. *Ibid.,* Act III, 11. 85–96 and 113–23.

32. "The Economy of Vegetation," Canto IV, 1. 408.

33. R. H. Fogle, *The Imagery of Keats and Shelley: A Comparative Study* (Hamden, Conn., 1962), first published 1949, is the source of this well-known contrast.

34. Some critics tend to read Darwin as a Neoplatonic visionary in associating him with Shelley: "Electricity, for example, something mysterious, a coruscant blue and green flame, elusively and unpredictably spirit-like, was more to the mind of an Erasmus Darwin or a Shelley than the colorless mechanics which Addison had supposed to be reality." W. K. Wimsatt, Jr., *Philosophic Words* (New Haven, 1948), p. 103.

35. Bernard Blackstone, *The Consecrated Urn* (London and New York, 1959), pp. 70–71. At the beginning of his book, Blackstone gives us an expressive image for Darwin's influence on all the Romantics: "I would like the reader to think of him [Darwin] as a churchyard yew, spreading

his wide branches in storm and sunlight over the more remarkable writers who follow him; overshadowing them, dropping an occasional cone, so to speak, into the pools of their verse." Blackstone, p. xiv.

36. Philip C. Ritterbush, *The Art of Organic Forms* (Washington, 1968), p. 19.

37. M. B. Forman, ed., *The Letters of John Keats,* 3rd edition (London, 1948), p. 7. To Charles Cowden Clarke, October 9, 1816.

38. See Alex Zwerdling, "The Mythographers and the Romantic Revival of Greek Myth," in *Publications of the Modern Language Association,* LXXIX (1964), 447–56. Blackstone says "Keats's temple [in Hyperion] may owe something to Darwin's," and then quotes from *The Temple of Nature.* Blackstone, p. 246.

39. Walter Jackson Bate, *John Keats* (Cambridge, 1964), p. 473.

40. *The Temple of Nature,* Canto II, 11. 299–304, and *The Eve of St. Agnes,* 11. 239–43.

41. King-Hele, p. 143.

42. Byron, *English Bards and Scotch Reviewers,* 11. 894–96.

43. For this interpretation of *Don Juan,* I am indebted to W. H. Marshall, *The Structure of Byron's Major Poems* (Philadelphia, 1962). Unfortunately, Professor Marshall does not mention Darwin.

44. Robert D. Hume, "Gothic Versus Romantic: A Revaluation of the Gothic Novel," in *Publications of the Modern Language Association,* 84 (March, 1969), 289.

45. The definitive biography of Byron contains only this: "Then on March 4 [1810] the English sloop-of-war, the *Pylades,* came into port at Piraeus. Captain Ferguson, accompanied by a tall young man, Dr. Francis Darwin, son of the author of *The Botanic Garden,* called and offered passage to Smyrna." [Byron went.] Leslie A. Marchand, *Byron, a Biography* (New York, 1957), p. 231.

46. Loren Eiseley, *Darwin's Century* (New York, 1961), first published 1958, p. 352.

Selected Bibliography

The following working bibliography is divided into three categories: primary sources of Darwin's writings, secondary sources of comment about Darwin's writing, and a third section of critical works about eighteenth-century and Romantic literature, not listed under category two, which have figured in my interpretation of Darwin's relation to his age. Although this is an annotated bibliography, I annotate some entries very briefly because their titles suggest why they are included or how important they are. In a sense, everything that has been written about eighteenth-century and Romantic literature is relevant to understanding even the smallest part of it, but the following list will help the student select what is most useful in understanding Erasmus Darwin.

PRIMARY SOURCES

Although comment about Darwin's writings continually appears, no complete scholarly edition of his work exists in print, and the scholar must rely on numerous old trade editions and modern facsimile reprints of these. Since a recent "selection" of his writing has just been published, I list first this modern reprint of his work, and then those original and facsimile editions that I used. For a complete listing of the many editions and translations of Darwin's books, see the fine bibliography in James V. Logan, *The Poetry and Aesthetics of Erasmus Darwin* (Princeton: Princeton University Press, 1936).

KING-HELE, DESMOND, ed. *The Essential Writings of Erasmus Darwin, edited with a linking commentary.* London: MacGibbon and Kee, 1968. Important selections from both the poetry and prose, but no substitute for a scholarly edition. Darwin is now and then included in modern anthologies, not always just surveys of literature. For instance, most recently 44 lines and notes from *The Botanic Garden* appeared in Allan Danzig, ed., *The Theme of the Machine.* Dubuque, Iowa: Wm. C. Brown, 1969.

The Botanic Garden, Part I, The Economy of Vegetation. London: J. Johnson, 1791. A facsimile reprint of the first edition from University Microfilms.

The Botanic Garden, A Poem in Two Parts. Third edition. London: J. Johnson, 1795.

The Botanic Garden, Part II, The Loves of the Plants. Fourth edition. London: J. Johnson, 1799.

The Botanic Garden, A Poem, in Two Parts. Second American edition. New York: T. & J. Swords, 1807.

Phytologia: or the Philosophy of Agriculture and Gardening. Dublin: P. Byrne, 1800.

A Plan for the Conduct of Female Education in Boarding Schools. With a new Preface. New York: Johnson Reprint Corp., 1968. First published 1797.

The Poetical Works. Three vols. London: J. Johnson, 1806.

"Remarks on the Opinion of Henry Eeles, Esq., Concerning the Ascent of Vapour," *Philosophical Transactions—Royal Society of London,* 50 (1757), 240-54.

The Temple of Nature; or, The Origin of Society: A Poem, With Philosophical Notes. London: J. Johnson, 1803. A facsimile reprint of the first edition from University Microfilms.

The Temple of Nature . . . . London:J. Johnson, 1803.

The Temple of Nature . . . . New York:T. & J. Swords, 1804.

The Temple of Nature . . . . London: Jones and Co., 1824.

"An Uncommon Case of an Haemoptysis," *Philosophical Transactions—Royal Society of London,* 51 (1760), 526-29.

Zoonomia; or, The Laws of Organic Life, vol. I. London: J. Johnson, 1794. vol. II. London: J. Johnson, 1796.

Zoonomia . . . . Third American edition. Two vols. Boston: Thomas and Andrews, 1809.

Secondary Sources

1. Commentary and Critical Studies of Darwin's Works

Anonymous Poetry of the Anti-Jacobin. Fourth edition. London: J. Wright, 1801. "The Loves of the Triangles," the famous parody of Darwin's poetry is in here.

Ashmun, Margaret. *The Singing Swan, An Account of Anna Seward and Her Acquaintance with Dr. Johnson, Boswell, and Others of Their Time.* New Haven: Yale University Press, 1931. Biographical and anecdotal detail; in addition, useful critical preface by Frederick Pottle.

Barlow, Lady Nora, ed. *The Autobiography of Charles Darwin, 1809–1882.* New York: Harcourt, Brace and Co., 1958. Surprisingly little mention of Erasmus Darwin, Charles's grandfather.

Bate, Walter Jackson. *From Classic to Romantic.* New York: Harper Torchbooks, 1961. First published 1946. Some discussion of Darwin's esthetic theories and their relation to eighteenth-century theories of literature.

Bates, Madison C. "Cowper to Hayley and Rose, June 1792: Two Unpublished Letters," *Harvard Library Bulletin,* XI (1957), 80–101.

Evidence to support Cowper's favorable reception of *The Botanic Garden.*

BLACKSTONE, BERNARD. *The Consecrated Urn, An Interpretation of Keats in Terms of Growth and Form.* London: Longmans, Green and Co., 1959. Lengthy and serious consideration of Darwin's poetry and its influence on the Romantics.

BRANDL, LEOPOLD. *Erasmus Darwins Botanic Garden.* Vienna and Leipzig: Wilhelm Braumuller, 1909. Mostly paraphrase and dated comment about Darwin's scientific ideas in the poem.

————. *Erasmus Darwin's (sic) Temple of Nature.* Vienna and Leipzig: Wilhelm Braumuller, 1902. Mostly paraphrase and dated comment about Darwin's scientific ideas in the poem.

BRONSON, BERTRAND H. "Personification Reconsidered," *Journal of English Library History,* XIV (1947), 163–77. Relates personification to the love of making categories; helps understand Darwin's use of personification.

BROWN, THOMAS. *Observations on the Zoonomia of Erasmus Darwin, M. D.* Edinburgh: Mundell and Son, 1798. Says that Darwin's materialism is a result of too much speculation. Darwin did not stoop to answer as Brown was just a university student at the time.

BUTLER, SAMUEL. *Evolution, Old and New.* London: Jonathan Cape, 1921. Sixth edition. An attempt to put forward Erasmus Darwin's theory of the inheritance of willed characteristics in evolution over against Charles Darwin's theories; generally a favorable reading of the energy and extent of the older Darwin's work.

CARLYLE, THOMAS. "Wordsworth's Poetical Works," *Fraser's Magazine,* VI (November, 1832), 607–25. Unsympathetic reading of Darwin's verse techniques by a disciple of Wordsworth.

CHAMBERLAIN, ROBERT L. "George Crabbe and Darwin's Amorous plants," *Journal of English and Germanic Philology,* LXI (1962), 833–52. Explains Crabbe's revision of *The Library* in 1807 to rid it of any taint from Darwin's radicalism.

CHAPIN, CHESTER F. *Personification in Eighteenth-Century English Poetry.* New York: Octagon Books, 1968. First published 1954. Valuable chapter discusses Darwin's poetic theory and theory of personification.

COLERIDGE, SAMUEL TAYLOR. *Biographia Literaria.* J. Shawcross, ed London: Oxford University Press, 1958. First published in this edition 1907. Coleridge uses Darwin as an example of bad writing.

————. *Shakespearean Criticism.* Thomas Middleton Raysor, ed. New York: E. P. Dutton, 1960. First published in this edition 1930. These lectures, of course, antedate the *Biographia;* and in these lectures Coleridge started using Darwin as an example of bad writing.

CREEGER, GEORGE R. and JOSEPH W. REED, JR., eds. *Selected Prose and*

Poetry of the Romantic Period. New York: Holt, Rinehart and Winston, 1964. Several good selections about Darwin from early nineteenth-century commentators on literature.

CRUM, RALPH B. *Scientific Thought in Poetry.* New York: Columbia University Press, 1931. Fairly superficial about Darwin's use of scientific ideas in poetry.

DARLINGTON, C. D. *Darwin's Place in History.* New York: Macmillan Co., 1961. Excellent discussion of early theories of evolution; fine chapter on Erasmus Darwin.

DEANE, C. V. *Aspects of Eighteenth Century Nature Poetry.* Oxford: Blackwell, 1935. Laughs at Darwin's couplet that calls a spade a metallic blade, and the like, but fails to identify where it comes from.

DONNER, H. W. *Thomas Lovell Beddoes, The Making of a Poet.* Oxford: Blackwell, 1935. Describes the way in which Dr. Beddoes, the father of T. L. Beddoes, imitated Darwin.

DRACHMAN, JULIAN M. *Studies in the Literature of Natural Science.* New York: Macmillan, 1930. Unsatisfactory understanding of Darwin's literary effects; discusses his work in relation to the literature of science.

DRINKWATER, JOHN. *A Book for Bookmen.* London: Dulau and Co., 1926. Favorable discussion, but treats Darwin as an eccentric.

EDGEWORTH, RICHARD LOVELL, *Memoirs of . . . . Third Edition,* London: Richard Bentley, 1844. Hyperbole from one of Darwin's friends. Edgeworth predicts that "in future times some critic will arise, who will rediscover *The Botanic Garden* and build his fame upon this discovery" (328).

EISELEY, LOREN. *Darwin's Century, Evolution and the Men Who Discovered It.* New York: Doubleday, 1961. Mostly biographical reference to Erasmus Darwin as Charles's grandfather.

ELLEGARD, ALVAR. *Darwin and the General Reader, The Reception of Darwin's Theory of Evolution in the British Periodical Press, 1859–1872.* Goteborg, Sweden: University of Goteborg, 1958. Mentions Erasmus Darwin's radicalism in passing.

ELTON, OLIVER. *A Survey of English Literature, 1780–1880.* Four vols. London: E. Arnold, 1912-20. One of the more balanced and thorough discussions in survey writing of Darwin's literary effects.

EMERY, CLARK. "Scientific Theory in Erasmus Darwin's *The Botanic Garden*," *Isis* XXXIII (September, 1941), 315–25. Treats inadequately the overall literary effect of the poem.

EVANS, MARY ALICE. "Mimicry and the Darwinian Heritage," *Journal of the History of Ideas,* XXVI (June, 1965), 211–20. Mentions *Zoonomia* as an antecedent to Charles Darwin's work, and as a kind of literary influence.

FUSSELL, PAUL, JR. *Theory of Prosody in Eighteenth-Century England.*

New London, Conn.: Connecticut College Press, 1954. Excellent general discussion; accurate in the brief mention of Darwin's prosody.

GARFINKLE, NORTON. "Science and Religion in England, 1790-1800: The Critical Response to the Work of Erasmus Darwin," *Journal of the History of Ideas,* XVI (June, 1955), 376–88. Describes the rapid rise of Darwin's literary reputation, and swift conservative reaction to his radicalism.

GLASS, BENTLEY, OWSEI TEMKIN and WILLIAM L. STRAUS, JR., eds. *Forerunners of Darwin, 1745-1859.* Baltimore: Johns Hopkins Press, 1968. First published 1959. Good for understanding the background of Erasmus Darwin's materialism; some mention of him.

GRABO, CARL. *A Newton Among Poets, Shelley's Use of Science in Prometheus Unbound.* Chapel Hill: University of North Carolina Press, 1930. Lengthy treatment of Erasmus Darwin's appeal to Shelley; too much emphasis on Darwin's belief in free will.

HASSLER, DONALD. "Amateur or Specialist" (review of *Erasmus Darwin* by Desmond King-Hele), *Canadian Forum,* XLIV (October, 1964), 168. Trying out of generalizations about Darwin.

———. "Coleridge, Darwin, and the Dome," *The Serif,* IV (September, 1967), 28–31. A possible source for "Kubla Khan."

———. "David Hume and Erasmus Darwin's *Zoonomia*," *Studies in Scottish Literature,* VIII (1971), 190–93. A note on the one reference to Hume in *Zoonomia.*

———. "Erasmus Darwin and Enlightenment Belief," *Enlightenment Essays,* I (1970), 77-83. More discussion of Darwin's belief of unbelief.

———. "Erasmus Darwin's Comic Bathos," *The Serif,* VI (June, 1969), 15-26. Much of the discussion of Darwin's comic literary effect that is reprinted here.

———. "The Poems of Erasmus Darwin." Unpublished doctoral dissertation. Columbia University, 1967. Goes much more fully into Darwin's stylistic devices in the use of the heroic couplet.

HOPKINS, KENNETH. *Portraits in Satire.* London: Barrie Books, 1958. In discussing "The Loves of the Triangles," expresses more admiration for Darwin's original verse that is being parodied.

HUNT, LEIGH. "Mr Keats's Poems, Literary Notices no. 30," *The Examiner* (June 6, 1817), 428–29. Laughs at Darwin's verse as an example of bad writing.

JONES, WILLIAM POWELL. *The Rhetoric of Science.* Berkeley and Los Angeles: University of California Press, 1966. Says that Darwin knew too much science to be a good poet and dismisses him.

KING-HELE, DESMOND. *Erasmus Darwin, 1731–1802.* New York: Macmillan, 1963. Good introduction to Darwin the versatile man inadequate discussion of the literary effects of his writings.

————. "The Influence of E. Darwin on Shelley," *Keats-Shelley Memorial Bulletin,* XIII (1962), 30–36. Fine discussion.

KRAUSE, ERNST. *Erasmus Darwin.* Translated from the German by W. S. Dallas with a preliminary notice by Charles Darwin. London: John Murray, 1879. Interesting anecdotes about Darwin's youth.

LEWIS, D. B. WYNDAM and CHARLES LEE, eds. *The Stuffed Owl, An Anthology of Bad Verse.* New York: Capricorn Books, 1962. First published 1930. Example of tendency to dismiss Darwin with a laugh.

LOGAN, JAMES V. *The Poetry and Aesthetics of Erasmus Darwin.* Princeton: Princeton University Press, 1936. A thorough and indispensable, if somewhat heavy, discussion of Darwin's literary production; a descriptive bibliography of the many early editions of his work.

LOWES, JOHN LIVINGSTON. *The Road to Xanadu.* New York: Vintage Books, 1959. First published 1927. Includes many references to Darwin as Lowes thinks Coleridge saw him.

LUCAS, E. V. *A Swan and Her Friends.* London: Methuen, 1907. Includes anecdotes about Darwin and Anna Seward.

MANIQUIS, ROBERT M. "The Puzzling *Mimosa*: Sensitivity and Plant Symbols in Romanticism," *Studies in Romanticism,* VIII (Spring, 1969), 129-55. Includes Darwin in a valuable historical discussion.

MONK, SAMUEL H. "Anna Seward and the Romantic Poets: A Study in Taste." E. L. Griggs, ed. *Wordsworth and Coleridge, Studies in Honor of George McLean Harper.* Princeton: Princeton University Press, 1939. Helpful in understanding the difference between Darwin and the Romantics; mentions Anna Seward's admiration for his work.

P. P. "A Review of 'The Economy of Vegetation,' " *Analytical Review;* or *History of Literature,* XV (March, 1793), 287–93. Favorable review; probably by Cowper.

PEARSON, HESKETH. *Doctor Darwin.* New York: Walker and Co., 1963. First published 1930. Adequate, helpful biography; too much emphasis on Darwin the eccentric; discounts him as a writer.

PIERCE, FREDERICK E. *Currents and Eddies in the English Romantic Generation.* New Haven: Yale University Press, 1918. Ridicules Darwin's awkwardness, which is described as "ponderous gambols of his great unpoetical mind like the mirth-provoking antics of Milton's elephant," (23).

PRIMER, IRWIN. "Erasmus Darwin's Temple of Nature: Progress, Evolution, and Eleusinian Mysteries," *Journal of the History of Ideas,* XXV (January—March, 1964), 58–76. Serious, extremely valuable, even seminal, discussion of Darwin's literary effects; includes discoveries about his use of myth and of the image of the circular return.

PRYCE-JONES, ALAN. "Erasmus Darwin," *London Mercury,* XX (July, 1929), 293-302. Most derogatory, snide treatment of Darwin to be read.

RENWICK, W. L. *English Literature, 1789–1815.* Vol. IX of the *Oxford History of English Literature.* Oxford: Oxford University Press, 1963. The account of Darwin is wrong in fact and depreciating in tone; says Pryce-Jones is best general appreciation.

RINGLER, RICHARD N. "The Genesis of Cowper's Yardley Oak," *English Language Notes,* V (September, 1967), 27–32. Says Cowper was influenced by writing a review of "The Economy of Vegetation."

RITTERBUSH, PHILIP C. *The Art of Organic Forms.* Washington: Smithsonian Institution Press, 1968. Provocative discussion of the influence of biology on art; gives Darwin more place than is usual in the history of ideas at the end of the eighteenth century.

————. *Overtures to Biology, The Speculations of Eighteenth-Century Naturalists.* New Haven: Yale University Press, 1964. Not so sympathetic to Darwin in this earlier book; gives his ideas lengthy consideration.

————. "Erasmus Darwin's Second Published Poem," *Review of English Studies,* XIII (1962), 158–60. Poem about shorthand quoted here.

ROSENFELD, ALVIN H., ed. *William Blake Essays for S. Foster Damon.* Providence: Brown University Press, 1969. Includes an essay on Erasmus Darwin and Blake.

ROSS, ROBERT N. " 'To Charm Thy Curious Eye': Erasmus Darwin's Poetry at the Vestibule of Knowledge," *Journal of the History of Ideas,* XXXII (1971), 379–94. Good on Darwin's esthetics.

RYSKAMP, CHARLES. "Cowper and Darwin's *Economy of Vegetation,*" *Harvard Library Bulletin,* XI (1957), 317–18. Attributes the two reviews in the *Analytical Review* to Cowper.

SAINTSBURY, GEORGE. *The Peace of the Augustans.* With an introduction by Sir Herbert Grierson. London: Oxford University Press, 1946. Unsympathetic to Darwin.

SCHIMMELPENNINCK, MARY ANNE. *Life of* . . . . Christiana C. Hankin, ed. Second edition. London: Longmans and Roberts, 1858. Relates how, as a little girl, she was terrified by their family friend, Erasmus Darwin.

SCHNEIDER, ELISABETH. *Coleridge, Opium and Kubla Khan.* Chicago: University of Chicago Press, 1953. Fine section on Coleridge's debt to Darwin.

SCHOFIELD, ROBERT E. *The Lunar Society of Birmingham.* Oxford: Oxford University Press, 1963. Account of Darwin's career; also a sensitive literary appreciation of his writing.

SEWARD, ANNA. *Memoirs of the Life of Dr. Darwin.* London: J. Johnson, 1804. Delightful account of Darwin's life and writing; prejudiced in his favor; some valid insights into his poetry.

SEWELL, ELIZABETH. *The Orphic Voice, Poetry and Natural History.* New Haven: Yale University Press, 1960. Includes Darwin with

Wordsworth and Goethe; takes his poetry very seriously; seminal study in any revaluation of Darwin.

SHAW, BERNARD. *Back to Methuselah, A Metabiological Pentateuch.* New York: Brentano's, 1921. Likes Darwin's energy and exuberance.

SPACKS, PATRICIA, ed. *Eighteenth Century Poetry.* New York: Prentice-Hall, 1964. In the introduction, Darwin suffers terribly at her hand as a whipping boy.

STEMPEL, DANIEL. "Coleridge and Organic Form: The English Tradition," *Studies in Romanticism.* VI (1967), 89–97. Describes Darwin's influence on Coleridge with regard to the notion of organic form and David Hume's influence on Darwin.

STEVENSON, LIONEL. *Darwin Among the Poets.* Chicago: The University of Chicago Press, 1932. Disparaging comments about Erasmus Darwin.

STIMSON, DOROTHY. *Scientists and Amateurs, A History of the Royal Society.* New York: Greenwood Press, 1968. First published 1948. Useful in understanding the "Transactions . . . ."

SYMONS, ARTHUR. *The Romantic Movement in English Poetry.* New York: E. P. Dutton, 1909. Another easy dismissal of Darwin.

TILLOTSON, GEOFFREY. *Augustan Poetic Diction.* London: The Athlone Press, 1964. Defends Darwin's use of thickly textured, garish language in a particular passage as expressive of the heavy, rich metals he is describing; a provocative close observation that is possible if Darwin is not dismissed outright.

VINES, SHERARD. *100 Years of English Poetry.* London: Duckworth, 1950. Closer to the Arthur Symons cursory treatment than to Geoffrey Tillotson's close observation (both mentioned above); not of much use.

WALPOLE, HORACE. *Correspondence.* W. S. Lewis, ed. Vol. XI. New Haven: Yale University Press, 1944. Enthusiastic about Darwin.
———. *The Letters of Horace Walpole, Fourth Earl of Oxford.* Mrs. Paget Toynbee, ed. Vol. XV. Oxford: Oxford University Press, 1905. The older edition of his letters.

WHITNEY, LOIS. *Primitivism and the Idea of Progress in English Popular Literature of the Eighteenth Century.* New York: Octagon Books, 1965. First published 1934. Primer corrects her overemphasis on Darwin's belief in progress.

WILLIAMS, HARLEY. *Great Biologists.* London: G. Bell and Sons, 1961. Simplified but accurate account of Darwin's theories in biology.

2. Background Studies for Darwin's Age

ABRAMS, M. H. *The Mirror and the Lamp.* New York: W. W. Norton, 1958. First published 1953. Mentions Darwin; most valuable as background for Romantic literary theory.

ARTHOS, JOHN. *The Language of Natural Description in* 18*th-century Poetry.* Ann Arbor: University of Michigan Press, 1949. Best work on eighteenth-century periphrasis I know.

BATE, WALTER JACKSON. *John Keats.* Cambridge: Harvard University Press, 1963. Helpful in doing careful literary analysis.

———. *The Stylistic Development of Keats.* New York: The Humanities Press, 1958. First published 1945. Sophisticated understanding of sound devices.

BECKER, CARL L. *The Heavenly City of the Eighteenth Century Philosophers.* New Haven: Yale University, 1932. Helpful for understanding *philosophes.*

BROWN, WALLACE C. *The Triumph of Form, A Study of the Later Masters of the Heroic Couplet.* Chapel Hill: The University of North Carolina Press, 1948. Helpful for rhetoric of the couplet.

BRYANT, JACOB. *A New System; or, An Analysis of Antient Mythology.* Third edition. London: J. Walker, etc., 1807. Darwin used Bryant extensively.

BUSH, DOUGLAS. *Mythology and the Romantic Tradition in English Poetry.* New York: Norton, 1963. First published 1937. Rather superficial treatment.

CAMERON, KENNETH NEILL. *The Young Shelley, Genesis of a Radical.* New York: Collier Books, 1962. First published 1950. Mentions Shelley's fascination with Darwin; could be listed under category two of this bibliography.

COHEN, I. BERNARD and HOWARD MUMFORD JONES, eds. *Science Before Nineteenth-Century Anthology.* London: Andre Deutsch, 1963. Good collection of scientific prose.

DANET, PIERRE. *A Complete Dictionary of the Greek and Roman Antiquities.* Compiled originally in French, by Monsieur Danet. Made English with the addition of very useful maps. London: John Nicholson, 1700. Darwin continually refers to this work.

FELLOWS, OTIS E. and NORMAN L. TORREY. eds. *The Age of Enlightenment, An Anthology of Eighteenth Century French Literature.* New York: Appleton-Century-Crofts, 1942. Basic text for students of the period.

FOGLE, RICHARD H. *The Imagery of Keats and Shelley.* Hamden, Conn.: Archon Books, 1962. First published 1949. Standard study.

FREDMAN, ALICE GREEN. *Diderot and Sterne.* New York: Columbia University Press, 1955. Useful in understanding the *philosophes.*

FRYE, NORTHROP. *A Study of English Romantism.* New York: Random House, 1968. Good on the tonal complexities in the extremes of Romanticism.

———. "Towards Defining an Age of Sensibility," *Fables of Identity,*

Studies in Poetic Mythology. New York: Harbinger Book, 1963. Provocative new view of Darwin's period.

GAY, PETER. *The Enlightenment: An Interpretation.* New York: Knopf, 1966. Invaluable in studying the *philosophes.*

GEER, RUSSEL M. *Introduction and translation of Lucretius. On Nature.* New York: Bobbs-Merrill, 1965. Good, general introduction to the materialistic monism of classical times that Darwin inherits.

GUTHRIE, W. K. C. *Orpheus and Greek Religion, A Study of the Orphic Movement.* London: Methuen, 1952. Information on the mystery religions.

HAGBERG, KURT. *Carl Linnaeus.* Alan Blair, tr. New York: E. P. Dutton, 1953. The Linnaean system of plant classification is used by Darwin.

HARPER, GEORGE MCLEAN. "Coleridge's Conversation Poems," M. H. Abrams, ed. *English Romantic Poets, Modern Essays in Criticism.* New York: Galaxy Books, 1960. Important for understanding Coleridge's verse techniques.

HARTMAN, GEOFFREY H. *Wordsworth's Poetry, 1787–1814.* New Haven: Yale University Press, 1964. Provocative study of Wordsworth's beliefs.

HASSLER, DONALD M. *"Marino Faliero,* The Byronic Hero, and *Don Juan," Keats-Shelley Journal,* XIV (1965), 55–64. Byron's comic tone underlaid by belief.

HAZARD, PAUL. *European Thought in the Eighteenth Century.* New Haven: Yale University Press, 1954. Standard study of *philosophes.*

HUME, ROBERT D. "Gothic Versus Romantic: A Revaluation of the Gothic Novel," *Publications of the Modern Language Association,* 84 (1969), 282-90. Suggestive study of Romantic literary techniques.

HYMAN, STANLEY EDGAR. *The Tangled Bank.* New York: Atheneum, 1962. Pioneer study of scientific writing as literature.

JONES, HOWARD MUMFORD. "Albrecht von Haller and English Philosophy," *Publications of the Modern Language Association,* XL (1925), 103–27. An important introduction to an eighteenth-century physiologist who influenced Darwin.

KING-HELE, DESMOND. *Shelley, His Thought and Work.* New York: Macmillan, 1960. General but useful.

LANGE, FREDERICK ALBERT. *The History of Materialism.* Translated by E. C. Thomas with an introduction by Bertrand Russell. New York: Humanities Press, 1950. First published without apparatus of this edition in 1865. Extremely detailed study.

MACLEAN, KENNETH. *John Locke and English Literature of the Eighteenth Century.* New York: Russell and Russell, 1962. First published 1936. This work and the Tuveson book (below) treat a topic that needs more study.

MANUEL, FRANK E. *The Eighteenth Century Confronts the Gods.* Cambridge

Harvard University Press, 1959. Best treatment of the revival of myth in eighteenth century.

MARCHAND, LESLIE A. *Byron: A Biography*. 3 vols. New York: Knopf, 1957. Standard, detailed biography.

MARSHALL, W. H. *The Structure of Byron's Major Poems*. Philadelphia: University of Pennsylvania Press, 1962. Useful for *Don Juan*.

MYLONAS, GEORGE E. *Eleusis and the Eleusinian Mysteries*. Princeton: Princeton University Press, 1961. Archaeologist's account of the mysteries.

NICOLSON, MAJORIE HOPE. *Newton Demands the Muse, Newton's Opticks and the Eighteenth Century Poets*. Princeton: Princeton University Press, 1946. Studies the changing attitude toward light in this poetry.

―――. *Mountain Gloom and Mountain Glory, The Development of the Aesthetics of the Infinite*. New York: Norton, 1963. First published 1959. Thorough account of one aspect of the change in taste after scientific revolution.

OWEN, W. J. B., ed. *Wordsworth's Preface to Lyrical Ballads*. Copenhagen: Rosenkilde and Bagger, 1957. Useful introduction.

PECKHAM, MORSE. "Toward a Theory of Romanticism," *Publications of the Modern Language Association*, LXVI (1951), 5-23. Important definition of Romantic effects.

POULET, GEORGES, *The Metamorphoses of the Circle*. Carley Dawson and Elliot Coleman, trans. Baltimore: Johns Hopkins Press, 1966. Provocative; very useful on the images of circles in several literatures.

REED, MARK L. *Wordsworth; the Chronology of the Early Years, 1770–1799*. Cambridge: Harvard University Press, 1967. Mentions Darwin in passing.

ROPPEN, GEORG. *Evolution and Poetic Belief*. Oslo: Oslo University Press, 1956. Mentions Darwin in passing.

SCHOLES, ROBERT. *The Fabulators*. New York: Oxford University Press, 1967. Fine ideas on the theory of the comic literary effect.

SEBEOK, THOMAS A., ed. *Style in Language*. New York and London: M. I. T. and John Wiley & Sons, 1960. Collection of essays; discusses various devices.

SUTHER, MARSHALL. *Visions of Xanadu*. New York: Columbia University Press, 1965. Contains summaries of other important criticism on Coleridge and suggestive new ideas.

TRAWICK, LEONARD M. *Backgrounds of Romanticism*. Bloomington: Indiana University Press, 1967. Useful collection eighteenth-century writings with a good introduction.

TUVESON, ERNEST LEE. *The Imagination as a Means of Grace, Locke and the Aesthetics of Romanticism*. Berkeley and Los Angeles: University of California Press, 1960. Controversial, but valuable to this study.

WARREN, AUSTIN. *Rage for Order, Essays in Criticism.* Chicago: University of Chicago Press, 1948. Essay on Pope is good background for why Darwin wrote.

WASSERMAN, EARL R. *Shelley's Prometheus Unbound, A Critical Reading.* Baltimore: John Hopkins Press, 1965. Invaluable study of the poem.

————. *The Subtler Language, Critical Readings of Neoclassic and Romantic Poems.* Baltimore: John Hopkins Press, 1959. Good on the intricacy of literary device.

————. "The Inherent Values of 18th-century Personification," *Publication of the Modern Language Association,* LXV (1950), 435-63. Plausible defense of this misunderstood device.

WILSON, MILTON. *Shelley's Later Poetry.* New York: Columbia University Press, 1959. Good on *Prometheus Unbound.*

WIMSATT, W. K., Jr. *Philosphic Words.* New Haven: Yale University Press, 1948. Good on prose style and science writing.

————. *The Verbal Icon, Studies in the Meaning of Poetry.* New York: Noonday Books, 1965. First published 1954. Invaluable study of literary artifice.

WIMSATT, W. K., Jr., and MONROE C. BEARDSLEY. "The Concept of Meter: An Exercise in Abstraction," *Publication of the Modern Language Association,* LXXIV (1959), 585-98. Rather technical but sound.

WOLF, A. *A History of Science, Technology, and Philosophy in the Eighteenth Century.* London: George Allen and Unwin, 1939. Best as a reference book.

WOODRING, CARL. *Wordsworth.* Boston: Houghton Mifflin, 1965. Some important critical insights.

ZWERDLING, ALEX. "The Mythographers and the Romantic Revival of Greek Myth," *Publication of the Modern Language Association,* LXXIX (1964), 447-56. Detailed research to show the widespread interest in myth.

Index